M000087311

HOPE
for
TODAY
and
TOMORROW

Other books by

DONNA S. THOMAS

Climb Another Mountain,
Warner Press 2000

Through the Eyes of Christ:
A Short-Term Missions Journal 2001,
Revised Edition 2008

Becoming a World Changing Family: Fun & Innovative Ways to Spread
the Good News,
Baker Books 2003, YWAM Publishing 2008

Faces in the Crowd: Reaching Your International
Neighbor for Christ,
New Hope Publishers 2008

The "Why not?" Factor: Chuck Thomas, Trailblazer,
MACU Press 2010

HOPE
for
TODAY
and
TOMORROW

JOURNAL

My Husband Is Gone.

What Do I Do Now?

DONNA S. THOMAS

ALL RIGHTS RESERVED. No part of this work covered by the copyright hereon may be reproduced, transcribed, or used in any form or by any means—graphic, electronic, or mechanical, including photocopying, recording, taping, Web distribution, or information and retrieval systems—without permission.

All Scripture quotations, unless otherwise indicated, are taken from the HOLY BIBLE, NEW INTERNATIONAL VERSION©. Copyright © 1973, 1978, 1984 International Bible Society. Used by permission of Zondervan. All rights reserved.

Scripture quotations marked (GNT) are from the Good News Translation—Second Edition. Copyright 1992 by American Bible Society. Used by Permission.

Scripture quotations marked (MSG) are from *THE MESSAGE*. Copyright by Eugene H. Peterson 1993, 1994, 1996, 2000, 2001, 2002. Used by permission of NavPress Publishing Group.

Scripture quotations marked (NLT) are taken from the *Holy Bible New Living Translation*, copyright 1996. Used by permission of Tyndale House Publishers, Inc., Wheaton, IL 60189 USA. All rights reserved.

Scripture quotations marked (TLT) are taken from the *The Living Bible*, copyright 1971. Used by permission of Tyndale House Publishers, Inc., Wheaton, IL 60189 USA. All rights reserved.

Scripture quotations marked (NKSV) are taken from the *Holy Bible New King James Version*, copyright 1982. Used by permission of Thomas Nelson Publishers.

Cover photo by Bruce A. Roberts, RQuest, LLC

Editorial Services by Karen S. Roberts, RQuest, LLC

Copyright © 2013 Donna S. Thomas
All rights reserved.
ISBN: 0979192021
ISBN 13: 9780979192029

DEDICATION

Thank you, Heavenly Father, for your special care in giving these, your daughters, hope for today and tomorrow.

Marilyn Stanley

Marcy Mays

Suzonne Kardatzke

Donnabelle Landey

Jean McQuay

Mary Muth

Judy Lymer

Barbara Bond

Ruth Bryson

Nova Hutchins

Carol Pagliaro

Mary Ann Bancroft

Kelly Stewart

CONTENTS

Additional Chapters

Title   Page

31: _____   _____

32: _____   _____

33: _____   _____

34: _____   _____

35: _____   _____

FOREWORD

I would not be loved in my current location if it were not for the actions and reach of Donna Thomas. She connected with my wife and me at a time of great questioning and confusion. This is the experience you have when you encounter someone who is led by the Holy Spirit and seeks to be used by God. Throughout her life, Donna has served others. Donna and her husband Chuck made it a habit to go beyond borders and push the boundaries to ensure that others got connected with Jesus. It is as simple as that.

I have witnessed the pain and sadness as well as the joy of Donna's journey as a widow. She is no less active, and in some ways more so, because of being on her own. No matter her surroundings, she seems to find a way to reach out to those who are alone and lost. There is simply something different about the experience when you are reading words written by someone who seems to know your very thoughts and feelings, particularly those you may have never shared with others. It is because of how she has lived her life that she has encountered so many different people and been required to experience so many deep and powerful emotions.

Donna Thomas' latest writing reveals a deep understanding of loss and grief. The book is written for widows, but the content will have value for others as well. It is actually an interactive journal that provides a path for widows to live life after losing their husband. The thoughts, feelings, and behaviors revealed in the grieving process are explored in the writing. The readers are provided ample opportunity to respond and explore their own life journey. There are many helpful words, constructive writing exercises, and thought-provoking narratives throughout. As she does in her life, she does not let you sit comfortably by as a spectator. She invites you to engage in your life, just as it is, which means dealing with the sadness of a significant loss and experiencing the joy of a life well lived.

There is no doubt this writing and journal will impact the lives of many widows. Donna's understanding of living life as a widow provides hope to those who may believe there is no more hope. I believe the writing and journal will be a transforming experience for any widow who reads and experiences it. It is clear after reading this latest work of hers that the adventures continue in her life. It has been enlightening and heart-warming to be part of her life for this particular season.

Gregory Hale, Ph.D., Psychologist
Indianapolis, IN

WORDS FROM A WIDOW

I first became acquainted with Donna perhaps ten years ago as I was attending world missions events with my late husband, David. Often Donna was there too. David introduced me to her. I liked listening to both of them talk about God's heart for all peoples to know Him, how to better equip and engage local churches in God's global mission, and how to help individuals better understand that God is a missionary God and the Bible is a missionary book. Mobilizing for missions was their heartbeat, and conversation was passionate and stimulating.

It became clear quickly to me that Donna was a woman in love with Jesus, and she had no greater joy than helping others know Him too. I read her autobiography, *Climb Another Mountain*. She and her husband, Chuck, were partners in ministry in the local church and pioneered opportunities to serve cross-culturally on short-term mission trips long before many were taking these trips. Chuck's passing was a great shock and loss for all who knew him.

As I spent more time with Donna, her deep love and respect for Chuck was evident. I also began seeing the pain and heartache she experienced as a widow. It was not a big surprise, therefore, when Donna was one of the first who came to my house and wrapped her arms around me the morning after my own husband, David, died suddenly. With tears glistening in her eyes, Donna identified with my abrupt loss and numbness even though it had been more than twenty years since her husband had gone to heaven.

In the past year I have read a dozen helpful books on grief, loss, and the sorrow that accompanies becoming a widow. Hope for Today and Tomorrow is different from any of them. In it Donna captures many of the emotions and changes that occur internally and externally when a woman becomes a widow. Because Donna kept a journal detailing her day-by-day walk as a widow that first year after Chuck went on to heaven, she has been able to draw material from it for the thirty chapters of this journal for widows. Like Donna, I too have found that writing my feelings and praying aloud my heartache have helped me address my grief in this first year without David.

Donna's book uniquely helps the new widow who might want to write but just does not know how to get started. In each chapter, she has written those first sentences for the reader on topics widows face as they move from grief into hope and provided ample space for the reader to pour out her thoughts and feelings. In addition, Donna has included relevant Bible verses throughout and a prayer at the end of each chapter.

What Donna has written is just enough and not too much to focus on. In doing so, she has helped provide comfort from the written Word and The Living Word, Jesus, who wants to become our closest Companion on this difficult journey that we cannot escape.

Thank you, Donna, for giving us widows a journal that is easy to read and use, that speaks simply and clearly to what we are experiencing, and that helps us cling to Jesus, who provides us hope for today and tomorrow.

Marcy Mays, widow of David L. Mays, who suddenly went to sleep in Jesus on January 2, 2012 Brownsburg, IN

ACKNOWLEDGMENTS

How thankful I am for special friends that have helped in the thoughts and prayers in this book. The roll of widow is not desired, yet it happens to all who outlive their husband. It is a sad and lonely time that caused me to feel compelled to formulate this journal as a help to give widows hope for today and hope for tomorrow.

What a special treasure to me is my friend Karen Roberts, a professional editor, who knows how to make a much better book than I can make. She is a gift from God.

I am also blessed by the input of other widows who have traveled this road, including Barbara Bond, LeMoine Ralston, Marcy Mays, Jean McQuay, Marilyn Barnes, and a host of others. The Lord certainly works miracles, enabling me to put this all together with the assurance it will be a strength and a blessing to many. Numerous times in the Bible we are told to care for the widows and orphans; therefore, this book is in your hands with the purpose to help you or for someone you can help.

I am blessed with my family and want to thank them for always standing by me. My three sons and their wives, Chuck and Sue, Paul and Dawn, and John and Nancy, are a great encouragement to me. And I am blessed with nine grandchildren who are always a blessing to me: Heather, Erin, Bryson, Allie, Michael, John, Morgan, Martin, and Nicole. The Lord gives us family, and how I praise the Lord for them. And I praise the Lord for his direction, his care, and the joy and strength he always provides.

PREFACE

I never dreamed I would lose my husband when I did and how I did. I'm guessing you didn't either with yours. We knew it happened to others but surely not to me, at least when it did. I have learned, contrary to what people may say, widows do not just "get over" losing a husband, but we do have to learn how to deal with it.

In my journey through grief, it seemed different emotions would jump into my face each day. Emotions I didn't really know how to deal with, but there they were. Fortunately I had started journaling a few years before my husband's death. After his death, I poured out my heart in letters to my Heavenly Father. Those letters were a relief and a blessing to me then, and I have discovered now as I go back and read them how Almighty God cared for me and carried me through all those times.

This journaling book is my gift to you to help you know that you are not alone, that whatever you are feeling is okay. It is a place where you can pour out your heart to God and know that he hears every word and is with you every day and every hour in your journey through grief. In it you will find excerpts from my letters to my Heavenly Father and prompts to help you write your own. As you write your thoughts to your Heavenly Father, you too will receive his special love and care. And yes, he does have his special plans *just for you.* Pray to him and listen to him as he leads you on in this new, strange phase of your life.

ABOUT THIS RESOURCE
Hope for Today and Tomorrow offers thirty chapters of reflections on widowhood. Each chapter, or topic, includes four or more writing prompts on different aspects of the chapter's topic along with suggestions for finding the help you need. The topics range from the immediate issues of widowhood through anniversaries of key events as well as facing holidays without your loved one.

Although the chapters are presented as a series, *there is no specific order for how to use them.* The topical organization allows you to find what you need, when you need it, journaling at the point of your need and not in any regimented order. Chapter material can be used over several days or perhaps even weeks as you experience the challenges that face you.

Chapter 1, as an example, opens with realizing all the emotions a new widow encounters at the death and loss of her husband. Questions are asked for you to respond to, enabling you to begin to express your feelings. Each of the remaining chapters addresses specific emotions and challenges. Some of the challenges and emotions are the new fears, loneliness, financial decisions, confusion, forgetfulness, lack of self-worth, no energy, not fitting in, anger, feeling cheated, and realizing the stages of life. Later chapters are about questions to God, questions to your husband, self-pity, handling special days alone, learning to lean on the Heavenly Father, looking for blessings, emptying your husband's closet, becoming a mechanic, learning to laugh again, finding a new purpose in life, comforting others, and moving forward with the Lord's hand in yours.

Everything is written in journal form with questions to answer and ample writing space, enabling you to think about how you wish to address these emotions and challenges in your life. Every chapter also encourages you to write one of your responses as a letter to your Heavenly Father.

No doubt your personal journey through grief into hope for tomorrow will include topics not covered specifically here. Chapters 31 to 35 are yours to write! Feel free to use the pages provided at the end of this journal for those special topics you need to write about and remember. The Table of Contents page includes space for you to add your titles along with page numbers.

GOD'S MESSAGE FOR YOU

It was only five days after my husband and I found out he had terminal cancer that I received a special message from the Lord. It was that beautiful verse in Jeremiah 29:11. "For I know the plans I have for you," declares the Lord, "plans to prosper you and not to harm you, plans to give you hope and a future." I certainly had no idea what those words meant for me at the time. It seemed so out of place. My husband died in just eighty-five days. I had a plaque made of that verse with the date January 19, 1992 on it. It has been on my wall ever since.

Now, twenty-one years later, I am totally amazed at all the plans the Lord has had for me. I never dreamed of the ways he would use me and bless me. He has had me write five books, and this is my sixth. He has had me help national Christian leaders in twelve countries and hold pastors conferences in eighteen countries. He has led me to many places to declare his message and share his good news. Above all, he has provided for my needs as a widow and kept me moving forward, even at my now "tender age" of eighty-five. Yes, he is my Heavenly Father, and he will "never leave us nor forsake us" (1 Kings 8:57).

God has a message just for you to hear as his plan for your future unfolds before you. Think of this resource as your travel journal. My prayer, as you use it, is that it will become a precious and personal record of your experiences as you open yourself to all that the Heavenly Father has planned for you.

"Whether you turn to the right or to the left, your ears will hear a voice behind you, saying, 'This is the way; walk in it.'" Isaiah 30:21

NUMB AND IN SHOCK

"When I am afraid, I will trust in you. In God, whose word I praise, in God I trust; I will not be afraid."

PSALM 56:3,4

FOR TODAY: How did this happen?

QUESTION TO CONSIDER: Who am I now, and what do I do?

A *widow*? This word is strange and terrifying. I don't like that word. No, I don't like that word. Don't call me "unmarried" either. These labels aren't for me. They are for somebody else. I'm still married. It's just that my husband isn't with me anymore. Now I am not a couple, just a ONE. This label is not what I expected. Our wedding vows were forever. "For better or for worse, in sickness and in health, for richer or for poorer" … oh my, and "till death do us part." But this separation is impossible. I never dreamed it would happen to me, to us.

How do I feel about all these changes and now the term widow?

_____

_____

_____

_____

_____

_____

_____

_____

_____

_____

_____

_____

_____

1

"Submit yourselves, then, to God." James 4:7

_____
date

People talk to me. But I don't remember who they are or what they said. Friends have brought food and filled my kitchen and freezer, but I don't know what it is or who brought what. I do remember I had to make decisions. Yes, decisions about the funeral, about the service, about the cemetery, about everything. And I was the one to make them, not my husband. I don't remember who came to the funeral. I don't remember much at all, but I do remember it all happened. And now he is gone. Now I am alone. Yes, so alone.

What do I remember? What decisions did I have to make? Who helped me?

_____

_____

_____

_____

_____

_____

_____

_____

_____

_____

_____

_____

_____

_____

_____

_____

_____

_____

_____

_____

_____

_____

_____

_____

_____

_____

_____

_____

_____

_____

_____

_____

_____

_____

_____

"Never will I leave you; never will I forsake you." Hebrews 13:5
"The Lord is my helper; I will not be afraid." Hebrews 13:6

_____

Let's see, what day is it? What am I supposed to do today? These days are so hard. I am overcome with tears at any moment. Everywhere I look I expect to see my beloved husband walking across the lawn, going into the living room, out in the garage. The hardest is knowing I will never ever see him again. I feel left out. No purpose, no reason, just marking off time.

I am in the midst of a great darkness. My soul hurts. Yet I know you are here with me, Father. I know you hold my right hand and are leading me through all of this pain. There will be light again someday. I will laugh again someday. People tell me I will dance again someday. Right now I am to just rest on you, trust you to lead and guide me, to let you be in charge. Father, help me with these feelings. Right now I feel like I don't know how to do anything without my husband.

Where do I start? What am I supposed to do now?

_____

_____

_____

_____

_____

_____

_____

_____

_____

_____

_____

_____

_____

_____

_____

_____

_____

_____

_____

_____

_____

_____

_____

_____

_____

_____

_____

_____

_____

_____

_____

_____

_____

_____

"I am worn out from groaning; all night long I flood my bed with weeping and drench my couch with tears." Psalm 6:6

———————

Yes, I am weak and weary, unable to take care of myself; but I know you, Heavenly Father, are caring for me. You will pull me out of the mire and set my feet on solid rock. You will dry my tears and hold me in your arms and enable me to go on. You are my hope, yes, and you are my future. My trust is in you. I cannot trust myself.

I do praise you, and I honor you. I love you, my Heavenly Father. I thank you for being my Father, my Jehovah Shama. Oh, I thank you and I need you. Stay close to me, I pray. Help me to know what I am supposed to be doing now.

Dear Heavenly Father, here I am, and I need you. Help me, I pray. This is my prayer:

————————————————————————————————

————————————————————————————————

————————————————————————————————

————————————————————————————————

————————————————————————————————

————————————————————————————————

————————————————————————————————

————————————————————————————————

————————————————————————————————

————————————————————————————————

————————————————————————————————

————————————————————————————————

————————————————————————————————

_____

_____

_____

_____

_____

_____

_____

_____

_____

_____

_____

_____

_____

_____

_____

_____

_____

_____

_____

Father, as I begin this strange journey, help me remember that you are my Heavenly Father and you will always be with me regardless. You made me, you blessed my marriage, and you are with me now. Help me trust in you and follow your plan for this stage of my life. Yes, Father, yes.

MY FEARS

"For I am the Lord, your God, who takes hold of
your right hand and says to you, 'Do not fear; I
will help you.'" ISAIAH 41:13

FOR TODAY: God will help me with all my fears.

QUESTION TO CONSIDER: How can I learn to trust that the Lord is
with me throughout my day, all the time?

I am consumed with fears. Yes, yes, afraid of everything. Of being
alone, of driving my car, of losing my way, of being with people, of not
being with people, of making decisions. If I will have enough money for
today, for this year, for life, if, if, if. Oh, what consuming fears.

Experiencing loss affects my head, my heart, my spirit. Fear, confusion, disorganization, and even a strange relief at times are just a few of
the emotions I feel. Now is the time I need to develop a support system.
A small group that will care for me and wants to help. A group that will
readily be with me if and when I have trouble. Friends and family. Yes,
I need a group, friends and family, who really care where I am and what
I am doing. I especially need this group to support me now.

*Here is my list of family members on whom I know I can depend, and
here is what each might provide in the way of support for me.*

_____

_____

_____

_____

_____

_____

_____

_____

_____

_____

_____

_____

_____

_____

_____

_____

_____

_____

_____

_____

_____

_____

_____

_____

_____

_____

_____

_____

_____

_____

_____

_____

_____

"I am still confident of this: I will see the goodness of the Lord in the land of the living." Psalm 27:13

I, Donna, remember well the fear that consumed me one month after my husband's death. I was at the Chicago airport, where I had been many times, but that time I felt so afraid, so alone, so unsure of myself. Would I find the right gate? Would I be able to board? When I arrived at my destination, would I be able to find my car? Did anyone know where I was? Did anyone care?

As I prayed, the Lord gave me peace and calm and his way to control my fears. On arriving home, I sat at my computer and listed all my relatives and friends that I knew really did care. Then I asked each one if I could send a message on email and my schedule for the next month—where I would be and what I would be doing. Their replies were such assurance.

I have been sending out a monthly letter to my support team for the last twenty-one years, and it is still a tremendous comfort. These dear people have helped me conquer my fears, and I am most grateful.

Here is my list of friends to send my monthly letter to.

_____

_____

_____

_____

_____

_____

_____

_____

_____

_____

_____

_____

_____

_____

_____

_____

_____

_____

_____

_____

_____

_____

_____

_____

_____

_____

_____

_____

_____

_____

_____

_____

"Wait for the Lord; be strong and take heart and wait for the Lord."
Psalm 27:14

_____
date

Strange fears, irrational fears keep jumping into my heart. Where do they come from? What can I do with them? Oh yes, I have my list of family and friends. I can share with them because these people really do care for me. Keeping them informed by notes or email is the easiest way for me to connect with them.

When I send them my plans and my schedule on a regular basis, can I also share my thoughts with them this way too? Yes, I can. I need them, and I know they will be with me in trouble and they will help me with their love and understanding. Yes, they care, and I need them. What a blessing to have not only the special support of the Lord wherever I go but also the support of family and friends.

Here are some of my fears. Who else can I add to my list of those who I can count on as part of my support team?

_____

_____

_____

_____

_____

_____

_____

_____

_____

_____

_____

_____

_____

_____

_____

_____

_____

_____

_____

_____

_____

_____

_____

_____

_____

_____

_____

_____

_____

_____

_____

_____

_____

_____

_____

_____

"The Lord is my rock, my fortress and my deliverer." 2 Samuel 22:2
"With your help I can advance against a troop; with my God I can
scale a wall." 2 Samuel 22:30

What a blessing to have the special support of the Lord wherever I go and to have this support from my family and friends. To put it simply, this support will alleviate many of my fears.

Pray each morning for the Lord to go with you wherever you go—to walk with you, and to ride with you in the car. These prayers will give you comfort and a feeling of security. Your Heavenly Father is with you all the time. Yes, all the time. What a rich blessing.

What are my plans for today? How will I take the Lord with me?

_____

_____

_____

_____

_____

_____

_____

_____

_____

_____

_____

_____

_____

_____

_____

_____

_____

_____

_____

_____

_____

_____

_____

_____

_____

_____

_____

_____

_____

_____

_____

_____

_____

_____

_____

_____

_____

_____

Oh Father, what a blessing you are to me. I know you are with me all the time, every moment, and you give me peace. Go with me today and help me feel your presence. Thank you for your love and your arms of comfort and care. Thank you, Father.

NOW ALL ALONE

"We also rejoice in our sufferings, because we know that suffering produces perseverance; perseverance, character; and character, hope. And hope does not disappoint us, because God has poured out his love into our hearts by the Holy Spirit, whom he has given us." ROMANS 5:3-5

FOR TODAY: Aloneness. I am all alone now.

QUESTION TO CONSIDER: Being alone and fear can go hand in hand. Where is my peace?

In Coleridge's poem "The Rime of the Ancient Mariner," the traveler cries, "Alone, alone, alone on a wide, wide sea. And never a saint takes pity on my soul in agony." I don't know the rest of that poem, but I certainly claim those words. They ring in my head. I have many friends, but where are they now? I could be sick or dead in my home and nobody would know. I could be driving to some city, never get there, and nobody would know. There is no one to report to, no one waiting. It makes me feel so alone. I am so lonely, so alone.

Father, here is why I need your presence with me now, today.

_____

_____

_____

_____

_____

_____

_____

_____

_____

_____

_____

_____

_____

_____

_____

_____

_____

_____

_____

_____

_____

_____

_____

_____

_____

_____

_____

_____

_____

_____

_____

_____

"By day the Lord directs his love, at night his song is with me—a prayer to the God of my life." Psalm 42:8

_____
date

What am I to do, Lord? Are you with me? Oh yes, I remember your Word says you will never leave me or forsake me. I want to claim that promise. I remember too you said you would send your Holy Spirit, the Comforter, to be with your disciples after you had to leave them. I need your Comforter now, yes, your Holy Spirit, Comforter and Counselor. Send me your Holy Spirit so I won't be alone today.

Who might come see me today? Anyone? Maybe I should go and find one of my friends. Or is there a meeting at church that I could attend? I need somebody to talk with. Lead me and help me find a friend to talk with, to be with today.

Maybe I could make a new friend if I go out to get my lunch. I could strike up a conversation with someone. Would that work, Father? Go with me and help me to see someone else who seems to need a friend. You said you'd be with me and lead me, so I am going to trust this to happen.

Just what are my options for today? Who and where?

_____

_____

_____

_____

_____

_____

_____

_____

_____

_____

_____

_____

_____

_____

_____
_____
_____
_____
_____
_____
_____
_____
_____
_____
_____
_____
_____
_____
_____
_____
_____
_____
_____
_____
_____

*"God is our refuge and strength, an ever-present help in trouble.
Therefore we will not fear, though the earth give way and the
mountains fall into the heart of the sea." Psalm 46:1-3*

_____
date

Sometimes I even feel abandoned by my children. Help me realize they care but they also have their lives to live. Besides, my family cannot always fill the void of my loneliness. I am to go to you, lean on you, and feel your presence wherever I am. You said to "Ask and you will receive, and your joy will be complete" (John 16:24). I am certainly asking for you to help me now with my loneliness.

So where are my options of places to go, people to be with? Maybe I can go to a restaurant and talk to a waiter. How do I do that? Or maybe I can find another woman sitting by herself. Teach me, lead me, and maybe I can help that person too. Oh Father, help me listen to you.

What are some things I can do to help my aloneness?

_____

_____

_____

_____

_____

_____

_____

_____

_____

_____

_____

_____

_____

_____

_____

_____

_____

_____

_____

_____

_____

_____

_____

_____

_____

_____

_____

_____

_____

_____

_____

_____

_____

_____

_____

"Let him have all your worries and cares, for he is always thinking about you and watching everything that concerns you." 1 Peter 5:7 (NLT)

_____

I need to come to you, Father. You are always with me. You will never leave me alone. Help me use my time and resist the temptation to do nothing. Help me "give thanks in all circumstances, for this is God's will for you in Christ Jesus" (1 Thessalonians 5:18). I still have a roof over my head and food on my table, for which I am thankful. Help me develop friendships, and especially help me recognize your presence wherever I am. Yes, you said, "I will never leave you nor forsake you"(Joshua 1:5). Oh, thank you, Father. Thank you for your presence and your love.

Here is my list of some of your blessings you have given to me.

_____

_____

_____

_____

_____

_____

_____

_____

_____

_____

_____

_____

_____

_____

_____

_____

_____

_____

_____

_____

_____

_____

_____

_____

_____

_____

_____

_____

_____

_____

_____

_____

_____

_____

Oh Father, your love, your care, your presence with me is so wonderful. You give me strength and purpose for today. I don't know about tomorrow, but I do know you are with me now, and my trust and my joy are in you.

DECISION TIME

"Whether you turn to the right or to the left, your
ears will hear a voice behind you, saying, 'This
is the way; walk in it.'" ISAIAH 30: 21

FOR TODAY: Choices, decisions necessary in this new stage of my life

QUESTION TO CONSIDER: How can I learn to make major decisions and not make mistakes?

Should I or should I not? Tomorrow maybe I can decide. What do my children think? What does someone else say? Why do I even have to make these kinds of decisions by myself? Why isn't my husband here to affirm my decisions? I used to be able to make decisions, but now I am having trouble. I need to be accountable to someone who will help me and understand. And someone to help me with my medical directives. Who can help me with his or her advice?

Now is not the time, I know, to rush into any major decisions. For those that must be made now, a good practice is to sleep on them for at least a week. Some decisions I may be able to put off until I have to make them. This is the time, however, to make a list of what I need to accomplish. And include on that list the alternatives, the good, and the bad. I must work on these on the days when I am stronger and not compelled to hurry.

What do I really need to think about now?

_____

_____

_____

_____

_____

_____

_____

_____
_____
_____
_____
_____
_____
_____
_____
_____
_____
_____
_____
_____
_____
_____
_____
_____
_____
_____
_____

*"Search me, O God, and know my heart; test me and know my anxious
thoughts. See if there is any offensive way in me, and lead me in the
way everlasting." Psalm 139:23, 24*

_____
date

Wait. Don't make the mistake of making financial decisions while you are still in shock. Wait. Those big medical bills are impossible to understand. Set them aside until you can go to the billing offices in person whenever possible. Sit down with the people there, and have them help you understand what the bills are all about. Don't pay them until you are absolutely sure what they are. Yes, absolutely sure.

Soon there will be a knock on your door or a phone call from someone you don't even know telling you that now that you are without your beloved, he or she is there to help you with your financial decisions. Don't listen! Close the door. Hang up the phone! Yes, hang up the phone. You are in no condition to understand what these strangers are saying or make a decision based on what they are offering. Plenty of people are out there looking for widows to get money from them, one way or another.

What decisions are really on my doorstep right now? Who can I trust to help me with them?

_____

_____

_____

_____

_____

_____

_____

_____

_____

_____

_____

_____

_____

_____

_____

_____

_____

_____

_____

_____

_____

_____

_____

_____

_____

_____

_____

_____

_____

_____

_____

"I cry aloud to the Lord; I lift up my voice to the Lord for mercy."
Psalm 142:1

_____

date

I, Donna, remember a call from a stockbroker at one of the investment firms where my husband dealt. He had a "sure deal" waiting for me. He was sure it would really increase in value quickly. And it was up to me to make the decision. Yes, I'll go for it, or no, not now. I was in no condition to take that risk although he said it wouldn't be a risk. My answer had to be no because I needed time and understanding before I could risk making that decision. Then another call from another broker came, trying to sell me a "sure thing." That is when I learned that it was not the time to even listen to those calls. I was in no shape to make reasonable and responsible decisions.

Making good investment decisions is a learning process, and "sharks" are always out there waiting for those in the midst of grief who cannot make responsible decisions. I must remember, don't make those decisions today. They can wait. I can wait. I must wait until I am ready.

How do I answer these people when they call or knock? Father, help me write out some answers so I'll be ready for them.

_____

_____

_____

_____

_____

_____

_____

_____

_____

_____

_____

_____
_____
_____
_____
_____
_____
_____
_____
_____
_____
_____
_____
_____
_____
_____
_____
_____
_____
_____
_____
_____

*"See, I am sending an angel ahead of you to guard you along the way
and to bring you to the place I have prepared." Exodus 23:20*

For peace of mind, I will make that list of the decisions that are waiting for me. Which ones are calling for my attention? Those that are not urgent, and most can wait, I will simply put aside. I must tell myself this is not the time to address them. There will be a time for each one, and I do have them on my list. Then, as the time approaches for a decision, I will find someone to listen to that particular problem, someone I can consult for the best decision. Who is that someone? One of my children, a close relative, a close friend, my pastor, a trusted person in my church?

Now is the time to make my list, pray over it, and put it aside for a later time—not now, maybe not next week or even next month. Just "later," when the Lord tells me it is time to consider some of those things on my list.

Who can I get to help me with each of these decisions? I will need different ones for these different problems.

_____

_____

_____

_____

_____

_____

_____

_____

_____

_____

_____

_____

_____
_____
_____
_____
_____
_____
_____
_____
_____
_____
_____
_____
_____
_____
_____
_____
_____
_____

Father, oh how I thank you that you are my Father, my Heavenly Father who cares for me, who leads me, who is all comfort and love for me. Here is my list of decisions waiting for me. Tell me how to answer them and when to respond. You are my hope, my strength, and my assurance.

CONFUSED

"But from everlasting to everlasting the Lord's love is with those who fear him, and his righteousness with their children's children—with those who keep his covenant and remember to obey his precepts."

PSALM 103: 17, 18

FOR TODAY: Confused

QUESTION TO CONSIDER: How can I "think" again as I used to?

Let's see, what day is this? What am I supposed to be doing? And who am I? How easy it is to lose my identity. I am no longer defined as a wife. I won't write housewife where a form asks for occupation. Relationships are very important to women. I had a wonderful relationship, and now it is gone. I've asked myself these questions before, gone over these issues in my mind many times. I really am in a fog of confusion.

Overload? That is where I am right now. My mind is going in circles. No, it's not going at all. Where did I put those important papers? They seem to have a life of their own. Where is …? I'd better look in the trash, as things just seem to jump in there on their own.

I feel so strange. Lord, my mind needs your attention. Here is a list of things that are bothering me.

_____

_____

_____

_____

_____

_____

_____

33

_____

_____

_____

_____

_____

_____

_____

_____

_____

_____

_____

_____

_____

_____

_____

_____

_____

_____

_____

_____

_____

"For God is not a God of disorder but of peace." I Corinthians 14:33

date

I have too much on my mind plus several levels of conscious thinking going on all at the same time. No, I am not myself. How long will it take for me to recover?

Indecisive? Is this who I am now? Is it a part of widowhood? I guess it is perfectly normal to be indecisive at this stage of my life. I have been a team player all these years with my husband, and I want to hear his side of the story. But he is gone. Things change. Yes, things change all the time, and sometimes it catches me off balance. So do I look forward now, or do I look backward?

Here are some of my frustrations. Little ones and big ones, they all bother me. Why?

_____

_____

_____

_____

_____

_____

_____

_____

_____

_____

_____

_____

_____

_____

_____

_____

_____

_____

_____

_____

_____

_____

_____

_____

_____

_____

_____

_____

_____

_____

_____

_____

_____

_____

"Peace I leave with you; my peace I give you. Do not let your hearts be troubled and do not be afraid." John 14:27

Until now my day focused on my husband. Now what is the purpose? Everything has changed. Nothing is the same. Oh, yes it is. I am still living in the same house. I still have the same family. I still have the same car. I am in the same neighborhood. Even so, everything seems different. And it is. Everything changed, and yet everything stayed the same. Confused? You know it.

This is the time for me to bow before the Lord God Almighty. He never changes. He is always there. He loves me and cares for me. I am his child, his special child, and he is with me all the time. Always!

Hear me, O Lord. This is what I want to tell you.

_____

_____

_____

_____

_____

_____

_____

_____

_____

_____

_____

_____

_____

_____

_____

_____

_____

_____

_____

_____

_____

_____

"He wakens me morning by morning, wakens my ear to listen like one being taught." Isaiah 50:4

_____

"When I said, 'My foot is slipping,' your love, O Lord, supported me. When anxiety was great within me, your consolation brought joy to my soul."
Psalm 94:18,19

"'Because she loves me,' says the Lord, 'I will rescue her; I will protect her, for she acknowledges my name. She will call upon me, and I will answer her; I will be with her in trouble, I will deliver her and honor her.'"
Psalm 91:14,15 (author alteration: he, him changed to she, her)

What a joy to claim these verses of Scriptures. I need love, now. I need consolation, now. I need to be protected, now. And the Lord God Almighty is right beside me with his arms of love around me.

How special the Lord is to me right now. Here is what I want to talk to you about.

_____

_____

_____

_____

_____

_____

_____

_____

_____

_____

_____

_____

_____

_____

_____

_____

_____

_____

_____

_____

_____

_____

_____

_____

_____

_____

_____

_____

_____

Oh Father, I need you and I claim these promises. How precious to be your child and to have your tender loving care. Help me think clearly and act according to your plan and your direction I pray.

SLEEP? HOW DO I SLEEP?

*"I will lie down and sleep in peace, for you alone,
O Lord, make me dwell in safety."*
PSALM 4:8

FOR TODAY: Cannot sleep

QUESTIONS TO CONSIDER: Why go to bed? Why stay in bed? Why get up?

That bed looks so huge and so lonesome. Night is forever. Which side do I sleep on? Why does it feel so strange? There is no future. It will never get better. There is no end. How can I endure? Why did he die and I live? Oh my, life has lost its meaning. It is always a shock just to go in my bedroom and realize it is totally mine and only mine. Maybe I wanted some of this space before he died, but I don't want it now. I have the whole closet now too, but that isn't my desire.

So it is 10 p.m., or is it 11 p.m.? When should I go to bed? My sleep isn't like it used to be. Why do I wake up and think about him? Why can't I have a great dream about him? Why can't I sleep like I used to?

My sleep is so different. What should I do about it, and whom can I talk to about it?

_____
_____
_____
_____
_____
_____
_____
_____
_____

41

_____

_____

_____

_____

_____

_____

_____

_____

_____

_____

_____

_____

_____

_____

_____

_____

_____

_____

_____

"When you lie down, you will not be afraid; when you lie down, your sleep will be sweet." Proverbs 3:24

_____
date

Breakfast alone feels like rejection. Why doesn't he come and have breakfast with me? I guess eating alone is something I must work on. Maybe I should take a walk first. Maybe I should eat breakfast on the deck instead of in the breakfast room.

Just how long will it take me to get over this grief thing? That's a silly question because widowhood is not a disease. It is not a sickness. It is a phase of life whether I like it or not. People tell me I won't "get over it." I must learn to live with it.

I will learn to plan my bedtime, choose my side of the bed, and find my reasons to get up in the morning. I will learn to plan my breakfast. These choices will all come in time, and how I'm feeling about them right now isn't my fault. It is a part of life.

Here is what comes to my mind when I lie in bed, when I decide to get up in the morning, and when I am having my breakfast.

_____

_____

_____

_____

_____

_____

_____

_____

_____

_____

_____

_____

_____

_____

_____

_____

_____

_____

_____

_____

_____

_____

_____

_____

_____

_____

_____

_____

_____

_____

_____

_____

_____

"Answer me when I call to you, O my righteous God. Give me relief from my distress; be merciful to me and hear my prayer." Psalm 4:1

_____
date

Father, I don't know how to sleep anymore, but I trust you will rest my body and calm my mind. I have heard that repeating Bible verses when I want to sleep will be a help. I can certainly try that. Sounds like a good idea because I especially need your Word in my heart in these days. Now would be a good time to memorize more of your Word. I will search for key verses to put in my heart.

I need your help, your comfort. Give me peace and a good night's sleep. Help me feel your presence and your peace through the whole night. And when I wake, help me know you will be with me through the whole day. I want to learn to greet each morning as a gift from you.

Here is a list of Bible verses I want to memorize.

_____

_____

_____

_____

_____

_____

_____

_____

_____

_____

_____

_____

_____

_____

_____
_____
_____
_____
_____
_____
_____
_____
_____
_____
_____
_____
_____
_____
_____
_____
_____
_____
_____

"For it is with your heart that you believe and are justified, and it is with your mouth that you confess and are saved." Romans 10:10

_____

date

How about meeting with you, Lord, first thing in the morning? That should help. I know you will be there waiting for me to talk with you and for me to read your words. Yes, you are helping me again with another part of learning to live without my dear husband.

What would you have me read to prepare my heart for our time together? Old Testament? New Testament plus Psalms? Devotionals? I want my heart to be ready to listen to you.

Here are my choices in preparing my heart for our time together.

_____

_____

_____

_____

_____

_____

_____

_____

_____

_____

_____

_____

_____

_____

_____

_____

_____

_____

_____

_____

_____

_____

_____

_____

_____

_____

_____

_____

_____

_____

_____

_____

_____

_____

_____

Here I am, Father, for our time together. It is so precious to me to meet with you each morning, just the two of us. I want to learn from you. I need to follow your direction in my life. I have my list of things to do, but I want to follow your list for me first. Help me learn to listen to you instead of doing all the talking. Yes, our time together is so precious.

MY WORTH NOW

7

"You did not receive a spirit that makes you a slave
again to fear, but you received the Spirit of sonship.
And by him we cry 'Abba Father.' The Spirit himself
testifies with our spirit that we are God's children."
ROMANS 8:15,16

FOR TODAY: Lack of self-worth

QUESTION TO CONSIDER: Who am I, and to whom does it matter?

My identity is Mrs., his wife. Now I am a ... ugh ... a widow, single, alone, unmarried. No, not me. I am Mrs. Thomas, Chuck's wife. I don't want to sign that paper that states I am unmarried. See, here is my wedding ring!

Okay, what am I to do today? Without him I don't know where to start. I am not needed now. Nobody wants me to cook. Nobody wants to know what I'm going to do all day.

My husband needed me and I needed him; but now I am not needed; well, not like I was. That automatic program of activity each day just isn't here anymore. I don't know what to do today, and I don't think anybody cares anyway.

What do you, Lord, want me to do today? After all, you are my Abba Father.

_____

_____

_____

_____

_____

_____

_____

49

_____

_____

_____

_____

_____

_____

_____

_____

_____

_____

_____

_____

_____

_____

_____

_____

_____

_____

_____

"I will instruct you and teach you in the way you should go; I will counsel you and watch over you." Psalm 32:8

I guess this is self-pity. Actually it feels pretty good, since I am just plain tired of coping. Self-pity is easier to take than other people's pity. After all, now I am the one to judge my days with success or failure. Right now my success rate isn't all that great. How many more changes will I have to accept? How many more crises will I have to face single-handedly? How can I do it all without him? Who am I to do it all alone now anyway?

Is it always going to be like this? How do I get out of these feelings and move forward? Well, I have to get through them. How can I do it? I need a new purpose in my life. The Bible says, "Forget the former things; do not dwell on the past. See, I am doing a new thing!" (Isaiah 43:18,19)

Okay, what are some of the things I should be considering about my identity, my self-worth? Here are my thoughts.

_____
_____
_____
_____
_____
_____
_____
_____
_____
_____
_____
_____
_____
_____
_____
_____
_____
_____
_____
_____
_____

" 'For my thoughts are not your thoughts, neither are your ways my ways,' declares the Lord. 'As the heavens are higher than the earth, so are my ways higher than your ways, and my thoughts than your thoughts.' " Isaiah 55:8,9

_____
date

I need to find someone I can help. That would keep me busy for a bit. If my life is all about grieving, something is terribly wrong. I remember the two commandments Jesus gave us, to love the Lord with all our heart and soul and strength and to love our neighbor as ourselves. Looks like it is time for me to find somebody to help. It would give me something to do and a reason to live. That's what I need, the joy of helping somebody.

Father, please lead me to where I can do something worthwhile and help another person. Hey, maybe even help another widow. Hold it! Erase that word *widow* and use "another woman who has lost her husband."

How do I go about finding someone to help? Where can I find another "woman who has lost her husband" so we can help each other?

Where do I start? Here are some thoughts.

_____

_____

_____

_____

_____

_____

_____

_____

_____

_____

_____

_____

53

_____

_____

_____

_____

_____

_____

_____

_____

_____

_____

_____

_____

_____

_____

_____

_____

_____

_____

_____

_____

_____

_____

_____

_____

"No eye has seen, no ear has heard, no mind has conceived what God has prepared to those who love him." 1 Corinthians 2:9

—————————
date

When I find someone hurting like me, someone who has lost her husband too, then what do I do? I remember times people came to me, and I wanted them to listen. I wanted them to ask me about my husband. Mention his name. Oh yes, use his name and tell me what a good man he was.

But then sometimes it is better for them just to be there, to listen, and to show me their love. Sympathy does help. I can certainly give that to others, since I know all the pain that goes with this new life. Yes, I can do it, and I do want to help another widow going through the same trauma that I am.

Lord, help me search for other women hurting like I am. Show me how to find them. Who are they? Where are they? Here are some ideas for finding them.

—————————————————————————————

—————————————————————————————

—————————————————————————————

—————————————————————————————

—————————————————————————————

—————————————————————————————

—————————————————————————————

—————————————————————————————

—————————————————————————————

—————————————————————————————

—————————————————————————————

—————————————————————————————

—————————————————————————————

_____

_____

_____

_____

_____

_____

_____

_____

_____

_____

_____

_____

_____

_____

_____

_____

_____

_____

_____

_____

_____

_____

Father, I know you have your plans for me. Help me listen and be ready to do whatever you direct me to do. You are my God and my reason for getting up in the morning and for going forward each day.

STAGES OF LIFE

"'For I know the plans I have for you,' declares the Lord, 'plans to prosper you and not to harm you, plans to give you hope and a future.'" JEREMIAH 29:11

"Many, O Lord my God, are the wonders you have done, the things you planned for us no one can recount to you; were I to speak and tell of them, they would be too many to declare."
PSALM 40:5

FOR TODAY: What is this idea called stages of life?

QUESTIONS TO CONSIDER: What are the different stages of life, and how do I value them?

O Lord, what is going on? What is happening? Help me understand. You are my strength and my hope. You will help me remember the past with joy and find a way to look to the future. I never dreamed I'd be living on without my husband. People tell me there are stages of life, and I am in a new one. This is a new idea to me.

I am beginning to realize there *are* stages to my life. I've lived through them, but I didn't really recognize them. Sure I remember being a little girl, living with my mom and dad and family. That was my first stage, *my childhood stage.*

I will recall as much as I can from the year I was born up to my teenage years. There were special, meaningful people and mentors for me. And there were thankful times and painful experiences. I remember ...

57

_____

_____

_____

_____

_____

_____

_____

_____

_____

_____

_____

_____

_____

_____

_____

_____

_____

_____

"I will lie down and sleep in peace, for you alone, O Lord,
make me dwell in safety." Psalm 4:8

_____
date

I remember my *teenager stage*. One day I thought I was an adult and the next day I felt like a little girl. These thoughts and feelings went back and forth. I remember learning to drive the car, and I remember my mom telling me what happens to girls and our growth patterns. School was the focus of my life in this stage, and there were both good days and bad days. It was a matter of me learning what the boundaries were and how to adjust to them.

I remember ...

_____

_____

_____

_____

_____

_____

_____

_____

_____

_____

_____

_____

_____

_____

_____

_____

_____
_____
_____
_____
_____
_____
_____
_____
_____
_____
_____
_____
_____
_____
_____
_____
_____
_____
_____
_____
_____

"For you have been my hope, O Sovereign Lord, my confidence since my youth. From birth I have relied on you, you brought me forth from my mother's womb. I will ever praise you." Psalm 71:5,6

_____
date

I remember my first job and having a great time with all those new experiences and decisions. I had to make so many decisions and also learn about consequences. This stage, the *young adult stage*, was certainly interesting and also challenging.

I remember ...

_____

_____

_____

_____

_____

_____

_____

_____

_____

_____

_____

_____

_____

_____

_____

_____

_____

_____

_____

_____

_____

_____

_____

_____

_____

_____

_____

_____

_____

_____

_____

_____

_____

_____

_____

_____

_____

"These commandments that I give you today are to be upon your hearts. Impress them on your children. Talk about them when you sit at home and when you walk along the road, when you lie down and when you get up." Deuteronomy 6:6,7

Then I remember having that special date and falling in love. Oh, that first kiss, and what an experience it was. And of course I remember when he asked me to marry him. Ours was a delightful courtship and a beautiful wedding. It was my *young married stage*.

I remember ...

_____

_____

_____

_____

_____

_____

_____

_____

_____

_____

_____

_____

_____

_____

_____

_____

_____

_____

_____

_____

_____

_____

_____

_____

_____

_____

_____

_____

_____

_____

_____

_____

_____

_____

_____

_____

_____

*"I thought about the former days, the years of long ago;
I remembered my songs in the night." Psalm 77:5,6*

_____

A few years later we were blessed with baby number one and the beginning of the *family stage*. Having babies was quite an experience. Learning how to be a mother wasn't easy, but it was worth it. A great time and such wonderful memories. Those precious times together, picnics, parties, vacations, ball games, church activities, scouts, report cards, and graduations.

I remember ...

_____

_____

_____

_____

_____

_____

_____

_____

_____

_____

_____

_____

_____

_____

_____

_____

_____

_____

_____

_____

_____

_____

_____

_____

_____

_____

_____

_____

_____

_____

_____

_____

_____

_____

_____

_____

_____

"Train a child in the way he should go,
and when he is old he will not turn from it." Proverbs 31:20

Then came the *empty nest stage*. This stage changed our lives and provided time to do many of the things we never had time for before such as vacations for just the two of us, special trips we couldn't afford before. It was a precious, enjoyable time. Time barriers weren't there. It was just the two of us. Great times. Times to play with our grandkids too. What precious times the two of us had together.

I remember ...

_____

_____

_____

_____

_____

_____

_____

_____

_____

_____

_____

_____

_____

_____

_____

_____

_____

_____

_____

_____

_____

_____

_____

_____

_____

_____

_____

_____

_____

_____

_____

_____

_____

"Enjoy life with your wife, whom you love." Ecclesiastes 9:9

_____
date

Precious memories. How special to remember so many of them.

_____

_____

_____

_____

_____

_____

_____

_____

_____

_____

_____

_____

_____

_____

_____

_____

_____

_____

_____

_____
_____
_____
_____
_____
_____
_____
_____
_____
_____
_____
_____
_____
_____
_____
_____
_____
_____
_____
_____

*"He who pursues righteousness and love finds life,
prosperity and honor." Proverbs 21:21*

But now this new stage, the *widowhood stage,* hits me right in the face. Or is it the bewildered stage? I don't like it. I never thought of this being part of life. I didn't realize this was a possibility ... but here it is. And now I have to deal with it, to learn about it, and see how I can work through it. This must be how a paraplegic feels. Nothing is like it used to be.

How soon can I move on with life and leave the past behind me? When is it okay to move ahead and not feel I am dishonoring my husband?

I do have the Lord with me now. Yes, the Lord Almighty is my help. He will help me work through this widowhood stage. I *will* find the plan the Lord has for me now. He does love and care for widows and orphans, so like it or not, I qualify. And he will help me find a future I can enjoy. Yes, he does have his special plans just for me in this stage too.

Father, what are your plans for me? What do you want me to do? Maybe some of those things I never had time for. Or is it helping others that really need my help?

What are some options for me to explore?

_____

_____

_____

_____

_____

_____

_____

_____

_____

_____

_____

_____

_____

_____

_____

_____

_____

_____

_____

_____

_____

_____

_____

_____

_____

_____

_____

_____

Oh dear Heavenly Father, how I thank you for your love and care over me. How special that you are with me in this unexpected time of my life. I do trust in you. I know you especially care for widows and orphans, and now I qualify. Thank you for being with me. Lead me on with the plans you have for me. I am yours to do your will, your way. Lead me, guide me, show me what you have planned for me. I am yours.

FORGETFUL

"But you, O Lord, are a compassionate and
gracious God."
PSALM 86:15

FOR TODAY: Forgetful right now

QUESTIONS TO CONSIDER: Why can't I remember what I said, to whom, when, where, and why? Why do I forget so many things? Why am I simply unable to recall past events that previously I remembered in detail?

Where did I put that electric bill that came in yesterday? I cannot remember where I put things. It seems as though I am misplacing everything. Am I paying all the bills I should? Now I am afraid I will forget. When someone says, "But you said ..." it adds to my confusion. I don't remember what I said, or for that matter what I did.

What happened to all those papers I had in my hand a minute ago? The check I am to take to the bank is not on the counter where I put it a few minutes ago. That form I was supposed to fill out and return last week is not on my desk where I put it three days ago. I must be losing my mind, or else these papers have a life of their own. They tell me my mind is on overload.

Oh Father, help me remember all of the things that I must take care of soon. Here is my list.

_____

_____

_____

_____

_____

_____

_____

_____
_____
_____
_____
_____
_____
_____
_____
_____
_____
_____
_____
_____
_____
_____
_____
_____

*"Show me your ways, O Lord, teach me your paths; guide me in your
truth and teach me, for you are God my Savior and my hope
is in you all day long." Psalm 25:4,5*

FORGETFUL

_____
date

I have to do many things I didn't have to do before. I have to make decisions without my husband's input. I know I am forgetting important things in the process. Am I going crazy? People tell me this is part of coping with my loss, my grief, and the fact that he just isn't here anymore.

This is certainly the time to write down everything. Yes, everything. I must keep records, keep a log of messages, of phone calls with names and numbers and what the calls are about. I must keep an updated list of necessary tasks. I must have a file drawer for all my records. I will need them at income tax time. Very important, I must keep a ledger of my expenses and income just to be sure I have all the facts straight. Oh, now I have to worry about tax time too.

Here are some things I should put on my list that I must take care of. And whom can I talk to about them?

_____

_____

_____

_____

_____

_____

_____

_____

_____

_____

_____

_____

_____
_____
_____
_____
_____
_____
_____
_____
_____
_____
_____
_____
_____
_____
_____
_____
_____
_____
_____
_____
_____

"Teach me your way, O Lord; lead me in a straight path."
Psalm 27:11

I hear this trauma makes people forget important things. I must accept this fact, write down everything, and organize my papers so they won't be lost. And I must always check my wastebasket before I take it to the trash.

Yes, I need a plan to keep records of those phone calls, bills, estate records, and other issues I am facing. I can't remember now like I used to. I hope I can again soon. But for now I will make a plan, my way, my plan. I may just start all over fresh instead of trying to use a way I did it before.

Here are my thoughts today on how to keep all these records and where I keep them, how to separate the ones that are really important from the ones that can wait a bit.

_____

_____

_____

_____

_____

_____

_____

_____

_____

_____

_____

_____

_____

_____

_____

_____
_____
_____
_____
_____
_____
_____
_____
_____
_____
_____
_____
_____
_____
_____
_____
_____
_____

"He gives power to the weak and strength to the powerless. Even youths will become weak and tired, and young men will fall in exhaustion. But those who trust in the Lord will find new strength. They will soar high on wings like eagles. They will run and not grow weary. They will walk and not faint." Isaiah 40:29-31

_____
date

I must not forget my grandchildren's birthdays. Some very important dates are coming up. This is the time to make a date book or a calendar for the whole year and write all the dates and important activities in it. It will be a big relief just knowing I am organized and will not forget what I must do and want to do for my family and friends.

Here is my list of all my family and their important days. I'm including my special friends as well.

_____

_____

_____

_____

_____

_____

_____

_____

_____

_____

_____

_____

_____

_____

_____

_____

_____

_____

_____

_____

_____

_____

_____

_____

_____

_____

_____

_____

_____

_____

_____

_____

_____

_____

Okay, Father. Help me maintain what I've started to do here. This is my new way of being organized for now. This is my prayer.

ENERGY? WHERE DID IT GO?

*"My God, my God, why have you forsaken me?
Why are you so far from saving me, so far from
the words of my groaning?"*
PSALM 22:1

FOR TODAY: No energy. Living in a black hole.

QUESTION TO CONSIDER: Why am I so tired?

No reason to do anything. No spirit to do it either. Everything is an effort. Too much effort. Why try? How do I fix the things he used to fix? Who will go to the doctor with me today?

A hole, a grave, with no way to climb out and no light, but still breathing. Still alive. Does it matter what I wear? What I look like? Who cares? What does it matter what happens in this world or here in my town? It doesn't matter to me now. Where is my hope, no future? I look at those around me and they are all the same. I am not the same. I feel cheated.

Father, here are my feelings. Listen to me, I pray, and show me how I can get out of this black hole.

_____

_____

_____

_____

_____

_____

_____

_____

_____

_____

_____

_____

_____

_____

_____

_____

_____

_____

_____

_____

_____

_____

_____

_____

_____

_____

_____

_____

"Even though I walk through the valley of the shadow of death, I will fear no evil, for you are with me; your rod and your staff, they comfort me."
Psalm 23:4

———————
date

Grief is a dark basement, a hole, a grave. How do I get out of this hole? Where are the stairs that I can find my way out? Is the sun still shining and coming up every day? I do know that the sun still exists. How do I find it again?

I can't think of anyone except me. I feel cheated. Why did my husband die and my friends still have their husbands? Is anyone else suffering like I am?

I remember when a friend lost her husband. He died so suddenly last year. What did she go through? Maybe I should contact her and find out what she is thinking and feeling. This grief is too hard to handle alone. I need some help. Maybe she has some answers for me. I must get out of this hole. There has to be a reason for me to get up in the morning.

Help me, Father, find another widow who I can talk with and who will be understanding and helpful. Right now I am thinking, where can I go to look for other widows?

—————————————————————————

—————————————————————————

—————————————————————————

—————————————————————————

—————————————————————————

—————————————————————————

—————————————————————————

—————————————————————————

—————————————————————————

—————————————————————————

—————————————————————————

—————————————————————————

_____
_____
_____
_____
_____
_____
_____
_____
_____
_____
_____
_____
_____
_____
_____
_____
_____
_____
_____
_____
_____

"O Lord, the God who saves me, day and night I cry out before you. May my prayer come before you; turn your ear to my cry." Psalm 88:1,2

_____

Sometimes talking with others about this pain is more than I can handle. I want to forget and just run away. But maybe just talking with a close friend is an answer. Someone who will help me deal with what I am feeling.

Since this stage I'm in is a part of living, there must be some help for me to find my way out of this present grief, some way to get out of this dark hole and get on with life. What are my options?

Wait. There is a Scripture passage that I need right now. Isaiah 54:4,5. "Remember no more the reproach of your widowhood. For your Maker is your husband—the Lord Almighty is his name."

Okay, Father, your Word says you are my husband, my heavenly husband. Really? So here are some questions I want to ask you.

_____

_____

_____

_____

_____

_____

_____

_____

_____

_____

_____

_____

_____

_____

_____

_____

_____

_____

_____

_____

_____

_____

_____

_____

_____

_____

_____

_____

_____

_____

_____

_____

_____

_____

_____

"The Lord himself goes before you and will be with you; he will never leave you nor forsake you. Do not be afraid; do not be discouraged."
Deuteronomy 31:8

_____
date

Amazing. The Lord Almighty is my husband! Oh, what a Scripture. I claim it! Wow, the Lord Almighty is now my husband. That means he cares for me. That means he walks with me. He listens to me. He is lifting me out of this dark hole. He is helping me see the sunshine again. How amazing that the Almighty God of the whole universe takes care of me, and he is my husband now. This Scripture is mine. It is precious. I will start each day with it, talking to my heavenly husband, the Lord God Almighty.

Oh, I thank you and I rejoice that I can talk with you, as I talked to my husband, knowing you care for me. I need your help and guidance in everything I do.

Now is the time to list all the blessings that are mine since the Lord God Almighty is my caretaker, my heavenly husband. Oh yes!

_____

_____

_____

_____

_____

_____

_____

_____

_____

_____

_____

_____

_____

_____

_____

_____

_____

Father, I can talk to you any time, and I know you are listening. You are always with me regardless as to where I am. You said you would never leave me or forsake me. You are an awesome God, and your care over me is priceless. Thank you for your love and care. Oh, I do need you every day, every minute. How I praise you and honor you, my Lord, my God.

FITTING IN

"I lift up my eyes to the hills—where does my
help come from? My help comes from the Lord,
the Maker of heaven and earth. The Lord will
keep you from all harm—he will watch over your
life; the Lord will watch over your coming and
going both now and forevermore."
PSALM 121:1,2,7,8

FOR TODAY: Fitting in with others is so different now.

QUESTIONS TO CONSIDER: Where do I sit in church? What do I do
on weekends and holidays?

Going to church is so different now. Where do I sit, and with whom
can I sit? This seems like all new territory. I feel isolated, alone: in a
sea of hundreds. I will make a call, a plan, and ask to sit with one of my
friends ahead of time. This will give me the peace and comfort I need.

What happened to my close friends? It is so hard to connect. When
I call, I get the feeling I am imposing or intruding on their plans. Some
whom I have known for years do not act as if they know me now. Even
some of my friends that are couples have dropped me now that I am
single. I never dreamed of this. This stage of life is so different. I can
collapse and be a basket case, or I can call on the Lord to give me ideas
and plans to build my today and tomorrow.

*Okay, I **will** make a list of options and possibilities for going to church.
Better to plan ahead than be caught without any plans at all.*

_____

_____

_____

_____

_____

89

_____

_____

_____

_____

_____

_____

_____

_____

_____

_____

_____

_____

_____

_____

_____

_____

_____

_____

_____

_____

_____

"I can do everything through him who gives me strength."
Philippians 4:13

date

What do I do on Saturday and Sunday afternoons and evenings? The phone doesn't ring, and here I am, wanting to do something, to be with someone. I've never had weekends like this before. And then there are holidays ahead. What do I do on Memorial Day, the Fourth of July, and Labor Day? These are days my husband and I used to do special things together. Now it looks like it is up to me to figure out how to fit in with others to celebrate them. Should I invite friends to my house to celebrate? Why not?

Before Memorial Day comes, I will plan a special outing, maybe a trip to a museum or war memorial. I guess it is my turn to plan and make it happen.

Here is my list of ideas for Memorial Day, Fourth of July, and Labor Day. I need to make a plan for each one of them for this coming year.

_____

_____

_____

_____

_____

_____

_____

_____

_____

_____

_____

_____

_____

_____

_____

_____

_____

_____

_____

_____

_____

_____

_____

_____

_____

_____

_____

_____

_____

_____

_____

_____

_____

_____

"Forget the former things; do not dwell on the past.
See, I am doing a new thing." Isaiah 43:18

_____
date

All holidays are going to need new, special attention. Maybe today I can plan a picnic or a dinner and invite a couple of my friends to celebrate the next one. I can take the initiative and make it a celebration after all. I will not just sit at home on that day and wonder what is going on. Oh, this decision is a hard one for me. It isn't easy, and it is so different.

Tell me what to do, Lord. Here is a list of my frustrations about what to do on weekends and holidays. I need your help to deal with them before I can make any plans.

_____

_____

_____

_____

_____

_____

_____

_____

_____

_____

_____

_____

_____

_____

_____

_____

_____

_____

_____

_____

_____

_____

_____

_____

_____

_____

_____

_____

_____

_____

_____

_____

_____

"Therefore do not worry about tomorrow." Matthew 6:34

date

It is time for me to act. The Bible tells me to "delight yourself in the Lord and he will give you the desires of your heart. Commit your way to the Lord; trust in him and he will do this" (Psalm 37:4,5). I will commit to these upcoming times I have listed to you, Lord, and work out a plan that will bless me and a plan that will bless others. Yes, I can do that and I will.

Order my steps Father, and prepare my way that I may serve you and have your blessings and joy. I will ...

_____

_____

_____

_____

_____

_____

_____

_____

_____

_____

_____

_____

_____

_____

_____

_____

_____

_____

_____

_____

_____

_____

_____

_____

_____

_____

_____

_____

_____

_____

_____

_____

_____

Yes, Father, I will make plans for my times, my Saturday times, my Sunday times, my vacation times, my holiday times. It takes courage, so give me your courage, your strength to move forward and make these special days ahead something to look forward to. Oh, thank you that you are with me everywhere I go. Oh, thank you that you will never leave me or forsake me. Oh, thank you that you are my strength and that you are my God, my loving Heavenly Father, my heavenly husband, the Lord Almighty.

CHEATED

*"He wakens me morning by morning, wakens my
ear to listen like one being taught ... Because
the Sovereign Lord helps me,
I will not be disgraced."*
ISAIAH 50:4,7

FOR TODAY: CHEATED. Why do I feel that way?

QUESTION TO CONSIDER: How do I celebrate my special days—
our anniversary, our birthdays—without my husband?

Why do other couples get to celebrate their wedding anniversary
and I don't anymore? Why did God let this happen to me? Why didn't
God stop this dreadful and hurtful time?

What about our anniversary? We, no, I am to celebrate our anniversary. Just how do I do that? I can have a pity party. I can get someone to
go with me on a trip. I can make a contribution to something both my
husband and I were interested in.

I, Donna, celebrated one wedding anniversary by sending funds to
help build a church in India called the Thomas Chapel, which gives me
joy.

Maybe I could do something again like that, or at least help. That
would be a lasting memorial. Our names might even be placed on it. Now
that would be a super way to celebrate. Hey, this can even get exciting.
Imagine that! Oh, now I am even looking forward to this anniversary.

*What are some of the ways, some of the things I can do to celebrate
my _____ wedding anniversary this year?*

_____

_____

_____

_____

_____

_____

_____

_____

_____

_____

_____

_____

_____

_____

_____

_____

_____

_____

_____

_____

_____

_____

_____

_____

_____

_____

_____

_____

_____

_____

"You will go out in joy and be led forth in peace; the mountains and hills will burst into song before you." Isaiah 55:12

date

Here is another challenge facing me. My birthday is coming soon. What do I do on this special day of mine? I don't need a gift. I need my husband, but he isn't available. What would he do for me if he were here? Maybe I should look at it as to what I would do for him for his birthday.

I choose to get through my birthday without feeling sorry for myself. I can take a friend out for lunch or a nice dinner. I can invite some friends over on my birthday without telling them what this special day means to me. Even have a cake but skip the candles. I can go shopping to find something that my husband would buy for me if he were with me. I can write a birthday card to me from him and tape it to my mirror.

Here is a list of some times that are important to me and some things I can do to celebrate them.

_____

_____

_____

_____

_____

_____

_____

_____

_____

_____

_____

_____

_____

_____
_____
_____
_____
_____
_____
_____
_____
_____
_____
_____
_____
_____
_____
_____
_____
_____
_____
_____
_____

"Praise be to the Lord, for he has heard my cry for mercy. The Lord is my strength and my shield; my heart trusts in him, and I am helped. My heart leaps for joy and I will give thanks to him in song." Psalm 28:6,7

And now there is another important day, the day of his death. This is an important day to me too. Oh, I remember that day. Remembering it is my way to honor him, to make this day special. His birthday, my birthday, our anniversary, his death day, all are important days to me. They may not mean anything to others, but they do to me. There are some people I can talk with today so we can remember together. That will help because they care too.

Here are the ones who remember that day. Just a phone conversation will be a blessing to me. I will call them. Just hearing their voices and what they remember will help.

_____

_____

_____

_____

_____

_____

_____

_____

_____

_____

_____

_____

_____

_____

_____

_____

_____

_____

_____

_____

_____

_____

_____

_____

_____

_____

_____

_____

_____

_____

_____

_____

_____

_____

_____

_____

_____

"I have learned to be content whatever the circumstances."
Philippians 4:11

_____
date

Now I really am a new person. I'm not the person I used to be, as now I am just me, alone. And it is my choice and my choice alone to make this a positive journey or a negative one. I have felt cheated with losing my husband, but now I must move forward. I can't fix the past, but I can work on having a positive and productive future. In this area of my forward journey, I will seek my Heavenly Father's help today, tomorrow, and every day.

As I look around at other women like me, what positive things, choices, and attitudes do I see and would like to claim for me? Father, help me .... What do you want me to change?

_____

_____

_____

_____

_____

_____

_____

_____

_____

_____

_____

_____

_____

_____

_____

_____

_____

_____

_____

_____

_____

_____

_____

_____

_____

_____

_____

_____

_____

_____

_____

_____

Here I am, Father, coming to you again for your guidance and direction. I pray that you will give me your inspiration as to something significant I can do to celebrate my wedding anniversary this year and to go forward with my life. I am listening to you and waiting for your answer. Use my mind, my thoughts to make this day a special celebration in your plans.

JUST PLAIN ANGRY

*"May the words of my mouth and the meditation
of my heart be pleasing in your sight, O Lord, my
Rock and my Redeemer."*
PSALM 19:14

FOR TODAY: Handling my emotions

QUESTIONS TO CONSIDER: What do I do with my anger, my depression, and my other emotions, including those that come as a result of the dumb things people say to me?

My emotions are always hovering over me. Yes, I know this is a stage of life and that my husband is forever gone. But I am angry, yes angry at being a widow. Why did God let this happen? This is not something I like. How do I move from anger and search for confidence and assurance? Is it okay to be angry now?

Here are some of the reasons I am angry.

_____

_____

_____

_____

_____

_____

_____

_____

_____

_____

_____

_____

_____

_____

_____

_____

_____

_____

_____

_____

_____

_____

_____

_____

_____

_____

_____

_____

_____

_____

_____

"How long must I wrestle with my thoughts and every day have sorrow in my heart?" Psalm 13:1,2

_____
date

Anger is a common emotion that accompanies grief. Anger can be directed toward others. It can also be directed toward God. Why did God let this happen? Why didn't he stop this terrible time for me? These questions are examples of anger directed toward God. In the Old Testament, David expresses his angry feelings about being forgotten to God. In Psalm 22:1 he says, "My God, my God, why have you forsaken me?"

Here is how my anger over my loss shows itself in my life. I do remember angry moments, angry times.

_____

_____

_____

_____

_____

_____

_____

_____

_____

_____

_____

_____

_____

_____

"Hear my cry, O God; listen to my prayer ... lead me to the rock that is higher than I." Psalm 61:1,2

_____
date

And yes, I am upset, no, angry with my husband. He has left me with all this mess, all these things he has kept over the years that are just plain trash. What am I to do with them? He should have used the wastebasket. It would have been so much easier on me than going through all his "stuff." If he was here now I would be angry with him. It is even worst for me to have to clean up not only his stuff but some decisions and lack of decisions that were his. Maybe it is good he isn't here right now so my anger will calm down.

These are the things that upset me about what he left me to deal with.

_____

_____

_____

_____

_____

_____

_____

_____

_____

_____

_____

_____

_____

_____

_____

_____

_____

_____

_____

_____

_____

"In your anger, do not sin. Do not let the sun go down while you are still angry." Ephesians 4:26

_____
date

Feelings of isolation and anger consume me at times. How do I handle them? Being alone in the grocery store is so different now. I always bought my groceries with my husband in mind. What would he like to eat? What could I fix special for him? And those special prices, two for the price of one, upset me now. I don't need that much. All the other customers seem so intent on what is on their list. Mine is so short now because I am not buying with my dear husband in mind anymore. All this just makes me upset, no, angry. I just poured a quart of milk down the drain because it soured before I could drink it. This makes me angry and sad.

Father, here is my list of things that upset me and make me angry.

_____

_____

_____

_____

_____

_____

_____

_____

_____

_____

_____

_____

_____

_____

_____

_____

_____

_____

_____

_____

_____

_____

_____

_____

_____

_____

_____

_____

_____

_____

_____

_____

_____

_____

_____

_____

"Be completely humble and gentle; be patient, bearing with one another in love." Ephesians 4:2,3

Oh, the dumb things people say sometimes. Like at a restaurant when the person to seat me asks, "How many?" and I have to say, "One." Too many times the next response is, "Only one?" I could hit these people for making me say it not once but twice, but they don't realize how their questions and my responses are so upsetting to me.

Sometimes in a group all the couples are asked to stand. That certainly leaves me out. Or someone tells me her mother died so she knows just how you feel? Really? She doesn't go to bed with her mother, get up out of bed with her every morning, eat all her meals together with her, or celebrate her wedding anniversary with her. Oh Father, I need your help in all these situations. Help me not to get angry. Teach me how to handle these encounters.

What are some ways for me to handle these encounters yet let people know they are hurting me with their words?

_____

_____

_____

_____

_____

_____

_____

_____

_____

_____

_____

_____

_____

_____

_____

_____

_____

_____

_____

"Love the Lord your God ... Love your neighbor as yourself."
Matthew 22:37,39

Ephesians 4:26 says, "In your anger do not sin. Do not let the sun go down while you are still angry, and do not give the devil a foothold." Galatians 5:22,23 says, "The fruit of the Spirit is love, joy, peace, patience, kindness, goodness, faithfulness, gentleness, and self-control." I do want to come through this process of grief with the right spirit and attitude. I have seen grumpy, complaining people, and I don't want to be one.

Father, here is where I need your help. How do I have the spirit of love? How do I have joy? Where do I find peace? I do want patience, kindness, goodness, and all of these special fruits of the Spirit. Oh please help me I pray.

What does it take to make me angry? Is my anger worth it? How can I become a more Christ-like person, filled with your spirit of love?

_____

_____

_____

_____

_____

_____

_____

_____

_____

_____

_____

_____

_____

_____

_____

_____

_____

_____

_____

_____

_____

_____

Father, I pray you will help me with my anger and how to handle these times when people are so hurtful. Help me to pray for them and forgive because they simply do not understand.

WHAT SHOULD I HAVE DONE?

"Hear my prayer, O Lord; let my cry for help
come to you. Do not hide your face from me
when I am in distress. Turn your ear to me; when
I call answer me quickly."

PSALM 102:1,2

FOR TODAY: Guilt, reliving the day he died, grief, pain

QUESTIONS TO CONSIDER: What did I do to deserve this? I must have done something to displease God for him to take my husband from me. What should I have done differently?

No one, yes, no one can ever understand the depth of my loss. I can't understand it either. It is beyond comprehension. What did I do to deserve it?

Everyone has to die. I understand that, but what could I have done to help him live longer? Did he get the care from me that he deserved? Did I give him the love he needed? Did I help him want to eat the right foods, want to exercise and take care of his body, want to cut down on stress?

Here are the thoughts about my husband's dying that are giving me trouble.

_____

_____

_____

_____

_____

_____

_____

_____

_____

_____

_____

_____

_____

_____

_____

_____

_____

_____

_____

_____

_____

_____

_____

_____

_____

_____

_____

_____

"As for man, his days are like grass, he flourishes like a flower of the field; the wind blows over it and it is gone, and its place remembers it no more." Psalm 103:15,16

———————
date

Oh, how I remember the day he died. What a day that was. Nothing like it before in my whole life and something I never, ever expected. How was I to know what that day would be like? I remember …. I remember ….

He was all the world to me. We had that beautiful relationship. And that day it ended. That was the end. He was dead. He couldn't respond. He couldn't hug me. He couldn't kiss me. He couldn't tell me he loved me. He was gone. Gone! Oh, I remember that feeling. I remember thinking it really wasn't happening. But it was, it did.

And now I am still here. All alone. I am still alive and working my way through this grief and pain. All by myself.

Oh, I remember. Yes, I recall each moment, each thought, each tear. Oh, I remember…

———————————————————
———————————————————
———————————————————
———————————————————
———————————————————
———————————————————
———————————————————
———————————————————
———————————————————
———————————————————
———————————————————
———————————————————

_____
_____
_____
_____
_____
_____
_____
_____
_____
_____
_____
_____
_____
_____
_____
_____
_____
_____
_____
_____

"Precious in the sight of the Lord is the death of his saints."
Psalm 116:15

WHAT SHOULD I HAVE DONE?

_____

date

Is a sense of guilt part of this mourning process? Do all widows have times of wondering if they did the right thing in caring for their husband? Did I feed him the right food? Did I encourage him to take care of his body? Did he go to the doctor for checkups when he should have? Did I ...?

Oh, it is easy to wonder what I could have done differently. Did he really need to go to that meeting or take that trip? Looking backward, I can find thoughts that overcome me. Is that what the Lord wants me to do, or should I turn my guilt over to him and ask for his forgiveness and for him to help me forget anything that I might have not done or done that wasn't helpful?

Here is my list of the good things I did for my husband and the special parties, surprises, dinners, and care I gave him. Yes, the good things, the special things.

_____

_____

_____

_____

_____

_____

_____

_____

_____

_____

_____

_____

_____
_____
_____
_____
_____
_____
_____
_____
_____
_____
_____
_____
_____
_____
_____
_____
_____
_____
_____
_____
_____
_____
_____

"God is our merciful Father and the source of all comfort.
He comforts us in all our troubles so that we can comfort others."
2 Corinthians 1:3,4 (NLT)

_____
date

I am beginning to discover there are other women that have gone through this same pain. I didn't realize it before. I didn't see their pain. Where was I when they were hurting? Now there are people around me that don't see my pain. They don't understand. I didn't understand until it hit me in my face.

I have gone blithely on my way, not realizing what others are going through. Now that I am going through it, I hope I can see others in pain and be there for them. Yes, Father, I trust I am learning what you want of me through all of this grief and pain. Yes!

Father, what are the things you want me to learn from the loss of my husband? What are you trying to teach me?

_____

_____

_____

_____

_____

_____

_____

_____

_____

_____

_____

_____

_____

_____

_____
_____
_____
_____
_____
_____
_____
_____
_____
_____
_____
_____
_____
_____
_____
_____
_____

Father, I surrender myself to you. You are my God, my Savior, and now my special husband. Oh, I pray you will give me your love and compassion for others that are going through this pain and loss too. Help me be a helper to you and share with them the love you have given me, the assurance that you are always with me and will never leave me. Yes, Father, I pray I can be useful to you in helping others with their pain and loss.

HIS CLOSET, HIS THINGS

———— ❧ ————

"For there is a proper time and procedure for
every matter." ECCLESIASTES 8:6

FOR TODAY: My dear husband's things

QUESTIONS TO CONSIDER: All around me are things that belonged
to my husband. What do I do with them now?

My husband's things are reminding me of him. His watch is lying on
the dresser. Beside it is his wedding ring. His shoes, his suits, his shirts
are hanging in the closet. They are precious to me, as these things were a
part of him. They smell like him too. Each one is a memory. Which ones
do I keep, and which ones do I give away? But I must wait. Not now. I
must wait for the right time. It doesn't have to be today or this month.

*I must make a list of all his things and what memories I have of them.
Here is the beginning.*

———————————————————————————————

———————————————————————————————

———————————————————————————————

———————————————————————————————

———————————————————————————————

———————————————————————————————

———————————————————————————————

———————————————————————————————

———————————————————————————————

———————————————————————————————

———————————————————————————————

"I will never leave you nor forsake you. Be strong and courageous."
Joshua 1:5b,6

_____
date

This task is important to me, and it is to be done with love and care. First, I will again just open the door and look and touch and smell. These are precious experiences, ones I want to remember. Second, I will make a list. It will help me know what I have so I can decide what I want to do with these things of his in due time, but not today.

What my dear husband wore and enjoyed is very important to me. But now that I think of it, who he was as a husband, a man who loved me, and as a follower of God, are even more important to me. Of course, he made some mistakes, and I have too.

Here are some of my favorite things he wore. Here is my list of some of the clothes and gifts he chose especially for me.

_____

_____

_____

_____

_____

_____

_____

_____

_____

_____

_____

_____

_____

_____

_____
_____
_____
_____
_____
_____
_____
_____
_____
_____
_____
_____
_____
_____
_____
_____
_____
_____
_____
_____
_____
_____

"For the eyes of the Lord are on the righteous and his ears are attentive to their prayer." 1 Peter 3:12

What all have I learned from having lived with him these years? What did he teach me to do and not to do? There were some difficult times, but together we came through them. Thinking back on these years together makes me see him in a more intimate light, even more special. Yes, first were years before we had children when it was just the two of us and we were young. What did I learn from him then? Then were those years together as a family with our children. He taught them as a father. I am so glad for all he was able to do before he died.

What three things did I learn from him during those times when our kids were growing up?

_____

_____

_____

_____

_____

_____

_____

_____

_____

_____

_____

_____

_____

_____
_____
_____
_____
_____
_____
_____
_____
_____
_____
_____
_____
_____
_____
_____
_____
_____
_____
_____
_____

"These commandments that I give you today are to be upon your hearts. Impress them on your children. Talk about them when you sit at home and when you walk along the road, when you lie down and when you get up." Deuteronomy 6:6,7

_____
date

I remember too our special times when it was just the two of us. We enjoyed our plans and our special times. He made some days so special for me. I want to remember where we went together. These memories are so precious.

I remember when just the two of us ...

_____

_____

_____

_____

_____

_____

_____

_____

_____

_____

_____

_____

_____

_____

_____

_____

_____

_____

_____

_____

_____

_____

_____

_____

_____

_____

_____

_____

_____

_____

_____

_____

_____

Father, how I thank you for those years you gave me with my dear husband. They were so precious. You have given me wonderful, special memories, and I remember them with joy and with pain. Yes, I call them sweet pain, and I do thank you for them.

LAUGH? HOW?

"We're depending on God; he's everything we need. What's more, our hearts brim with joy since we've taken for our own his holy name. Love us, God, with all you've got—that's what we're depending on."

PSALM 33:20–22 (MSG)

FOR TODAY: Learning to laugh again

QUESTIONS TO CONSIDER: How can I laugh again? How can I feel joy like I used to again?

This loss is so consuming. I can remember times when we were happy and joyful. I can remember times when we were laughing and having a good time. But they are all gone. How can I laugh now? What will it take for me to be happy now? I don't know. It is a new challenge for me. I'm not an upbeat person in this stage of life. It is a melancholy time.

The apostle John tells says in his book about Jesus that we will grieve, but our grief will turn to joy. And the apostle Paul tells us to be joyful always and pray continually. How can I do that? Show me, Father, that I can give you thanks in all circumstances. Help me, to begin to do it now. I need your help, and I want to laugh again and be joyful.

What can I do now that might help me rediscover what it means to be joyful and laugh again?

_____

_____

_____

_____

_____

_____

_____

_____

_____

_____

_____

_____

_____

_____

_____

_____

_____

_____

_____

_____

_____

_____

_____

_____

_____

_____

_____

_____

_____

"Always be full of joy in the Lord. I say it again—rejoice! "
Philippians 4:4 (NLT)

LAUGH? HOW?

_____
date

I have lost the meaning of joy, the feeling of happiness, and laughter. Does joy mean feeling good all the time? That's impossible! Not when I've lost my dearly beloved.

Father, give me something to be joyful about. And teach me, help me, show me how to find joy. When will it be okay to laugh again? How can I do it?

Here is what I want. Here is what I need today and tomorrow.

_____

_____

_____

_____

_____

_____

_____

_____

_____

_____

_____

_____

_____

_____

_____

_____

_____

_____

_____

_____

_____

_____

_____

_____

_____

_____

_____

_____

_____

_____

_____

_____

_____

_____

_____

_____

"Shout with joy to the Lord, all the earth. Worship the Lord with gladness; come before him with joyful songs. For the Lord is good and his love endures forever; his faithfulness continues through all generations." Psalm 100:1,5

As I study and search the word of God, I am discovering that joy is the settled assurance that God is in control of everything in my life—all the details, the good things, and the things that hurt. I can find in his Word that he cares for every detail of my life. He even says he takes care of the birds of the air and the lilies of the field, and he says we are so very much more important than they are. There it is in Matthew 6:25–34, just waiting for me to claim it. Oh, I must learn to claim that promise.

Joy is the quiet confidence that God is in control of every bit of my life, the assurance that ultimately everything is going to be all right, and the understanding he will help me praise him even in this stage of my life. Joy includes the knowledge that even though this time in my life is so painful, Almighty God loves me and will give me his joy and the wonderful experience of laughter again.

Here are the reasons I want joy again. Help me find the confidence that you are in control of my life, you love me, and you want me to laugh again.

_____

_____

_____

_____

_____

_____

_____

_____

_____

_____

_____

"And my God will meet all your needs according to his glorious riches in Christ Jesus." Philippians 4:19

_____

I must start thinking of others and what it takes to make them happy. If I can make one of my friends happy, it could put a smile on her face. And if I put a smile on her face, I can smile again too. If I can give her joy, I will have joy too. If I can hear her laugh, I can laugh again too.

I have the right to choose my attitude. I choose joy. Yes, Father, I choose joy. And I WILL laugh again.

Here is my list of some people I can help now.

_____

_____

_____

_____

_____

_____

_____

_____

_____

_____

_____

_____

_____

_____

_____

_____

_____

_____

_____

_____

_____

_____

_____

_____

_____

_____

_____

_____

_____

_____

_____

_____

Oh Father, knowing you are with me gives me strength. Knowing the trials of Jesus gives me assurance that regardless of all this pain, you are with me and you will again give me joy and enable me to laugh again. Yes, Father, let me learn to laugh in your presence while I am blessed by your company and your love. Oh, thank you that I can again have the strength that comes from you and the joy and purpose that you have for me all the days of my life. I praise you. I worship you. Help me see now who I can help, who needs my attention and care. You are my God, and you have your special plans just for me.

QUESTIONS TO GOD

—— ❧ ——

"Out of the depths I cry to you, O Lord; O Lord,
hear my voice."

PSALM 130:1,2

FOR TODAY: My questions to God

QUESTIONS TO CONSIDER: Why did he have to die? What is he doing now? What do you have for me to do now, Father, that my dear husband is gone?

Here is a fiction story about connecting to God through Skype.

I hurriedly pulled up the Internet to connect with my friend in Texas through Skype, the program that lets you talk to and see the person you are communicating with. I had used Skype before, and this time I was in a hurry. I only had a limited time to talk. So I worked quickly to make the connection.

I must have done something wrong because all of a sudden, a strange but beautiful and soft voice answered. "Hello, may I help you?"

"Huh, well, yes please. I am calling for Samuel in Texas. Who am I talking to?" I asked.

"I am an angel of the Lord."

"What? I beg your pardon. What did you say? The Lord? An angel?"

"Yes, I am an angel of the Lord. You have reached heaven. Do you want to talk to someone here?"

"Heaven? I have reached heaven on my computer?"

"Yes, I am an angel of the Lord, and I will help you. Who would you like to talk with?"

"Wow, you've got to be kidding. I was calling Texas, and I got you in heaven? How did this happen?"

"I will be happy to connect you to whomever you would like to talk with."

"Well, I want to ask God why my husband died. I never dreamed of anything like this. May I ask him some questions? Actually I have tons of questions. Can I really talk to God, Almighty God? Is this real?"

"Of course, you can talk to God. He always wants you to talk with him. So go ahead and ask God questions. He is your Heavenly Father, and he is waiting to talk to you."

Now is the time. Here are some questions that are on my heart and in my mind.

_____

_____

_____

_____

_____

_____

_____

_____

_____

_____

_____

_____

_____

_____

_____

_____

"Give ear to my words, O Lord." Psalm 5:1

I have some more questions. Can I talk to my mother, who is there with you now too? Besides this, would it be possible to talk with your disciple John? He was instructed to take care of Jesus' mother at the crucifixion. How did he do that?

I have been searching in the Bible for more information on heaven. John wrote that Jesus was going to heaven to prepare a place for us. What does this mean? Also, Jesus said he is the way and the truth and the life. No one comes to the Father except through him. If I follow Jesus, will I make it to heaven? Help me find the answers to my questions and to put my total faith in you.

Yes, Father, here are more of my questions. Why did ...? What can I expect now that ...?

_____
_____
_____
_____
_____
_____
_____
_____
_____
_____
_____
_____
_____
_____
_____
_____
_____
_____
_____
_____
_____

"This is love for God; to obey his commands. And his commands are not burdensome, for everyone born of God overcomes the world."
1 John 5:3,4

_____
date

I have some unusual questions too. I would like to ask Jonah if it was slimy inside the whale. I have a question for Peter too, since Matthew 8:14 tells us he had a mother-in-law. Did he have children? What did his wife say about him being gone all the time? How did Jesus feel when the rich young ruler turned his back on him and left him? And how in the world do you feed 5,000 people plus women and children out on a hillside? I would even like to ask Martin Luther how much courage it took to nail that manifesto on the chapel door. My friend's baby died four hours after birth. Did he grow up, or is he still a baby?

Father, what is heaven like? What do you have ahead for me? Do you really have a mansion for your children? Are the streets made of gold, or is this just the only way we can imagine anything as wonderful as heaven? Who all can I see and talk with?

Here is what I imagine heaven must be like.

_____

_____

_____

_____

_____

_____

_____

_____

_____

_____

_____

_____

_____

_____

_____

_____

_____

_____

_____

_____

_____

_____

_____

_____

_____

_____

_____

_____

_____

_____

_____

"I will come back and take you to be with me that you also may be where I am." John 14:3

More questions? My Heavenly Father is listening. He knows the pain in my heart, he knows the questions in my mind, and he cares about all that has happened to me. Of course, I live in a sin sick world, and there is trouble everywhere. This is why he sent his Son Jesus, to give me hope, faith, and confidence that he loves me regardless and will take care of me until it is time for me to be with him forever.

I have poured out my soul to you, Father. I have shared my pain with you My grief hurts, and it is always with me. But now I want to affirm that you are such a tremendous blessing to me. You are always with me and care for me. Through all of my pain and sorrow, you have held my hand. You are caring for me in every situation. Let me list the ways and the places and the times I have felt your special care for me. How precious you are to me.

_____

_____

_____

_____

_____

_____

_____

_____

_____

_____

_____

_____

_____
_____
_____
_____
_____
_____
_____
_____
_____
_____
_____
_____
_____
_____
_____
_____
_____

Awesome, Father. To think I can connect with you on Skype. But better yet to actually know I can connect with you anytime, anywhere. You are an awesome God, and you care for the widows and orphans especially. Oh, wow, I bow before you to honor you, to worship you, and to listen to your instructions for me. I want to be faithful to you with all that is within me. How I thank you for your directions, your instructions, and your walk with me in this journey through life,. You are an awesome God.

QUESTIONS TO MY HUSBAND

18

"Come to me, all you who are weary and burdened, and I will give you rest." MATTHEW 11:28

FOR TODAY: My questions to my husband

QUESTIONS TO CONSIDER: If I can ask my Heavenly Father questions, can I ask my husband questions too? And especially, can I just tell
him how much I miss him and what a blessing he was to me?

Okay, I am still on Skype, this is still fiction, but now I am talking
with my loved one. It feels so real. Yes, now is the time to talk to my
precious husband and ask questions. Here are a few of my words to him
and my questions.

I miss you so much, but I wouldn't call you back to this
world. Our world is getting weird.
Guess what I put on your tombstone?
Do you miss me?
Do you know how much I miss you?
When I come home, I still call your name. Do you hear me?

*If I were talking to my husband, here are the first words I would say to
him and the first questions I would have for him.*

_____

_____

_____

_____

_____

_____

_____

_____
_____
_____
_____
_____
_____
_____
_____
_____
_____
_____
_____
_____
_____
_____
_____
_____
_____
_____
_____
_____

"I call on you, O God, for you will answer me; give ear to me and hear my prayer. Show the wonder of your great love." Psalm 17:6,7

I'm still on Skype. More questions to my husband.

>   Do you know what I am doing?
>   Are you helping good things come to me?
>   Do you know which side of our bed I sleep on?
>   Do you watch where I go and what I do each day?
>   What year was it we went to …?
>   Remember our wonderful vacation to …?
>   What should I do with all those tools of yours?
>   Who should I get to fix the gutters?
>   Is our house insurance okay?
>   How much do you miss me and our kids up there in heaven?

I'm listening. If you could really talk with me, what would you tell me?
Let me guess your answers, what you would want to say to me. Oh, how
I want to hear you say these words.

_____

_____

_____

_____

_____

_____

_____

_____

_____

_____

_____

_____

_____

_____

_____

_____

_____

_____

_____

_____

"Husbands, love your wives, just as Christ loved the church and gave himself up for her." Ephesians 5:25

More questions to my husband.

What is heaven like? Do you have a mansion? Who do you see? Do you see my mother and dad and your mother and dad? Who do you talk to?

What does Jesus really look like? What does he say to you?

Have you seen any of his disciples? Or David, or Isaiah, Martin Luther, or John Wesley?

Are there lots of people there? Do you know them? How do you know their names?

Here are a few more questions I want to ask you.

_____

_____

_____

_____

_____

_____

_____

_____

_____

_____

_____

_____

_____

_____
_____
_____
_____
_____
_____
_____
_____
_____
_____
_____
_____
_____
_____
_____
_____
_____
_____
_____
_____

"God has given us eternal life, and this life is in his Son." 1 John 5:11

date

More questions still.

    How do you function without "time" as we know it?
    What do you do in heaven?
    Are you looking over the balcony of heaven and helping me with my plans? I want to be able to look up to see if you are waving to me.

What a blessing to communicate with you. I know you are there. Here is what I want to do when I get to heaven with you.

_____

_____

_____

_____

_____

_____

_____

_____

_____

_____

_____

_____

_____

_____

_____

Father, I am so grateful for the dear husband you gave me. Our times together were so precious. You helped us in every situation, even when we saw things differently. Oh, I praise you, and now I thank you that you have my dear husband with you and he is enjoying all that is happening in heaven.

A NEW PURPOSE IN LIFE

— ❧ —

"The Spirit makes you God's children, and by
the Spirit's power we cry out to God, 'Father! My
Father!'" ROMANS 8:15B,16 (GNT)

FOR TODAY: I must find a new purpose for my life.

QUESTION TO CONSIDER: What should my purpose be now that I
am "single" and my life is so different than it was?

You are my Father, my Abba Father, and you are with me all the
time and everywhere I go. What I want to do today is to please you, to
be useful to you. Didn't you say you had your plans for me, plans to
prosper me and not to harm me? Plans to give me hope and a future?

Knowing you have a plan and a purpose for me gives me assurance
that you really do watch over me and care for me. I need to make my
mission statement now so I can focus on following your plan. Help me
think about how to write it and follow it to be useful to you.

Here I am, use me, I pray. What do you have ahead for me today?
This is a totally different life now with you as my heavenly husband, my
Heavenly Father, and my provider. Now I am to focus on your purpose,
your mission for me.

*Here are some of the things I think you might want me to focus on today
to please you and to serve you.*

_____

_____

_____

_____

_____

_____

_____

_____

_____

_____

_____

_____

_____

_____

_____

_____

_____

_____

_____

_____

_____

_____

_____

_____

_____

_____

_____

_____

_____

"You love me! You are holding my right hand! You will keep on guiding me all my life with your wisdom and counsel; and afterwards receive me into the glories of heaven!" Psalm 73:23,24 (TLB)

_____
date

Living with purpose is the only way to live. What should my purpose be? What do I want to accomplish in these days and years ahead? More importantly, who does God want me to be and do? My mission statement will help me direct my thoughts and actions today and in all my future. Yes, I have years ahead of me. What should I do in these years, what should I accomplish, and how can I best serve the Lord?

Here is my mission statement, my purpose in life, for as many years as I have yet to live.

_____

_____

_____

_____

_____

_____

_____

_____

_____

_____

_____

_____

_____

_____

_____

_____
_____
_____
_____
_____
_____
_____
_____
_____
_____
_____
_____
_____
_____
_____
_____
_____
_____
_____
_____

"For my thoughts are not your thoughts, neither are your ways my ways, declares the Lord." Isaiah 55:8

Here I am, at this special age and now a widow. How many more years will you give me? When I am older and look back over my life, what legacy will I have left? What legacy do I want to leave? How many people can I introduce to you and help them find you for their Savior, their provider, and their answer to life? Who am I to help?

Listening to you, I realize I don't have to do things the same way they have always been done. You will give me new ideas, new thoughts, new ways of serving you. When people come to me, help me to see them and recognize they are from you. Help me respond as you want me to respond. I know I can go forward with joy as you lead me and put in my heart to respond, "Yes, Father. Why not?"

Here are some new ideas you, Father, are you putting in my heart.

_____

_____

_____

_____

_____

_____

_____

_____

_____

_____

_____

_____

_____

_____

_____

_____

_____

_____

_____

_____

_____

"Whether you turn to the right or to the left, your ears will hear a voice behind you, saying, 'This is the way; walk in it.'" Isaiah 30:21

Okay, Father. Here is today. I have my list, but I want to know what is on your list for me. As I read your Word, I see that not everyone was ready when you called. Jonah certainly wasn't, and it took an interesting twist for him to realize you had a special job for him (Jonah 1 & 2). The apostle Paul was on the wrong road, and you changed his direction (Acts 9).

I want to be ready for your direction and to listen to your plans for me. This is a new life. A new beginning. A new journey into the future. I pray my ears will hear what you tell me and my heart will be responsive to your plans. You have chosen me and prepared me for this new adventure with you.

Here is what I will try today to begin living out my mission statement.

_____

_____

_____

_____

_____

_____

_____

_____

_____

_____

_____

_____

_____

_____

_____

_____
_____
_____
_____
_____
_____
_____
_____
_____
_____
_____
_____
_____
_____
_____
_____
_____
_____
_____
_____
_____

Father, my ears are listening. Yes, I am working on my new purpose in life. I don't want to be a "runaway Jonah." And I don't want to run ahead of you. I want your direction, your timing, and I certainly want you to be with me every day, every minute of my future. Your plans and your being with me will make my days joyful again. And different. Lead me on, Father, lead me on. This is my prayer.

WHAT ABOUT ME?

— ❧ —

"Love the Lord your God with all your heart and
with all your soul and with all your mind and with
all your strength. The second [commandment] is
this: Love your neighbor as yourself." MARK 12:30,31

FOR TODAY: My wedding ring, dinners, self-pity

QUESTIONS TO CONSIDER: Do I still wear my wedding ring? How
do I enjoy a meal both at home and in a restaurant when I am by myself?
How do I get over these feelings of self-pity and lack of value? Or am I
simply in a stage and the Lord will bring me through it?

I can make the choice to wear my wedding ring or not wear it. The
choice is mine. My dear husband gave it to me, and I have worn it all
these years. It belongs to me. It is mine. Father, thank you for giving me
this choice. It may give me some opportunities to tell others about my
husband and about the way you are caring for me now. Thank you that I
can still make choices and decisions. After all, why not?

Yes, these are the reasons I am still wearing my wedding ring.

_____

_____

_____

_____

_____

_____

_____

_____

_____

_____

_____

_____

_____

_____

_____

_____

_____

_____

_____

_____

_____

_____

_____

_____

_____

_____

_____

_____

_____

_____

"He has taken me to the banquet hall, and his banner over me is love." Song of Songs 2:4

Mealtime! Different now. I have to learn how to handle meals by myself. It is easier to eat in the kitchen than to sit at the table, but I don't think that is the best thing for me. Some times I feel I am just "going through the motions," exerting no enthusiasm, no feelings. Just there.

I need wisdom to choose my diet and eat what I should for good health and energy. I must learn to take care of myself as I should. Does this mean exercise too? A fitness class? I need advice in choosing what is best for me and the direction I should go.

What are some of the choices I need to make now to be strong and healthy?

_____

_____

_____

_____

_____

_____

_____

_____

_____

_____

_____

_____

_____

_____
_____
_____
_____
_____
_____
_____
_____
_____
_____
_____
_____
_____
_____
_____
_____
_____
_____
_____
_____
_____
_____
_____
_____

"Commit to the Lord whatever you do, and your plans will succeed."
Proverbs 16:4

———————————
date

It is so easy to think no one else understands what I am going through. No one else knows all this pain and the loss of that dear husband of mine. It seems that every breath I take and every thought I have is about me. I am self-absorbed, and it turns into self-pity. I have never admired anyone consumed by self-pity. Yes, I am grieving. Yes I have lost so much. How do I get out of this place and move on?

What can I be thinking about that is not about me? How do I learn to see others instead of focusing on myself?

———————————————————————————————
———————————————————————————————
———————————————————————————————
———————————————————————————————
———————————————————————————————
———————————————————————————————
———————————————————————————————
———————————————————————————————
———————————————————————————————
———————————————————————————————
———————————————————————————————
———————————————————————————————
———————————————————————————————
———————————————————————————————
———————————————————————————————
———————————————————————————————

_____

_____

_____

_____

_____

_____

_____

_____

_____

_____

_____

_____

_____

_____

_____

_____

_____

_____

_____

_____

_____

_____

"Because the Sovereign Lord helps me, I will not be disgraced."
Isaiah 50:7

_____
date

Father, I need your help now to move forward, to quit thinking so much about myself, and to follow your command to love you and love my neighbor. It is going to take your help and your strength. Come, Lord Jesus, and help me be who you want me to be.

How can I spread the Good News to others that Jesus is the one who gives real joy, real hope for the future? That he alone satisfies the longing, the big hole left in widows' hearts?

_____
_____
_____
_____
_____
_____
_____
_____
_____
_____
_____
_____
_____
_____
_____
_____

_____

_____

_____

_____

_____

_____

_____

_____

_____

_____

_____

_____

_____

_____

_____

_____

_____

_____

_____

_____

_____

Father, here I am. You gave us two commandments. The first is to love you, the Lord our God. The second is to love our neighbor. Help me to see my neighbor, those in need of you, those that are hurting, and those that don't know how loving and caring you really are. Yes, give me eyes to see what you see and words to help them. This is my prayer.

MY HEAVENLY FATHER

"Come to me, all you who are weary and burdened, and I will give you rest...I am gentle and humble in heart, and you will find rest for your souls."
MATTHEW 11:28, 29

FOR TODAY: Learning how to lean on my Heavenly Father

QUESTIONS TO CONSIDER: What do I do to lean on my Heavenly Father?

I can't ask my husband, but yes, Lord, you are my husband now and my caretaker, my advisor. I can ask you for help, for advice. Tell me what I should be doing and how to do it your way.

When do you want me to start meeting with you? And how often too? Do you want me to spend time with you each day? When should that be? The first thing in the morning or in the evening or when? What Scriptures do you want me to read to prepare for our time together? Do you want me to write a note to you each day? Oh, and teach me how to listen to you and follow your instructions.

What are my options as to a special time? Where is the best place? And how should I prepare for these times?

_____
_____
_____
_____
_____
_____
_____
_____
_____
_____

_____

_____

_____

_____

_____

_____

_____

_____

_____

_____

_____

_____

_____

_____

_____

_____

_____

_____

_____

_____

"I call on you, O God, for you will answer me; give ear to me and hear my prayer. Keep me as the apple of your eye; hide me in the shadow of your wings." Psalm 17:6,8

——————
date

Father, if I make this special time and learn to listen to you, will you give me special blessings? Can I learn to see your blessings and your care? I think I should be grateful for your closeness and your presence during all these difficult days of grief and mourning. I need to consider the things that make my life worth living and seek the possibilities you have for me of joy and love each day. Here is my morning song to you. I will add my own tune to it.

This is the day the Lord has made for me,
This is the day for me to serve thee,
Order my steps and prepare the way
For me to serve you this whole day.

Father, how do you want me to serve you today? What do you have in mind for me? Here are some of the options I see. What am I missing?

_____

_____

_____

_____

_____

_____

_____

_____

_____

_____

_____

_____

_____

_____

_____

_____

_____

_____

_____

_____

_____

_____

_____

_____

_____

_____

_____

_____

_____

_____

_____

"Trust in the Lord with all your heart and lean not on your own under-standing; in all your ways acknowledge him, and he will make your paths straight." Proverbs 3:5,6

_____
date

I still have much to be grateful for. Yes, my physical health, my family, my friends, and even the concern of strangers. And Father, I can be grateful for this very moment, as we are together and you are coaching me and leading me to inner peace and comfort.

I will start keeping a blessings journal. Yes, each night before I turn out the light, I will recount my blessings of the day. It will help me remember and see that I am making progress.

What were my blessings yesterday? What are my blessings today?

_____

_____

_____

_____

_____

_____

_____

_____

_____

_____

_____

_____

_____

_____

_____

_____

_____

_____

_____

_____

_____

_____

_____

_____

_____

_____

_____

_____

_____

_____

_____

_____

_____

_____

_____

_____

"Before I was born the Lord called me; from my birth he has made mention of my name." Isaiah 49:1

"In the Garden"

I come to the garden alone,
While the dew is still on the roses;
And the voice I hear, falling on my ear,
The Son of God discloses.
He speaks and the sound of His voice
Is so sweet the birds hush their singing.
And the melody that He gave to me
Within my heart is ringing.

Chorus:
And He walks with me,
And He talks with me;
And He tells me I am His own.
And the joy we share as we tarry there,
None other has ever known.

(C. Austin Miles, 1912, The Rodeheaver Co.)

A closeness to God is built on sharing everything with him. I must meet with him at a special time every day. And just as importantly, I must include him in every thing I do, every conversation, every problem, and every thought. I must not expect perfection on my part. What he wants is obedience, not necessarily success. I am to be his at all times and listen for his direction.

Father, here is how I feel today about the sound of your voice and our time together.

_____

_____

_____

_____

_____

_____

_____

_____

_____

_____

_____

_____

_____

_____

_____

_____

_____

_____

_____

Here I am alone with you, Father. This is a precious time for me. The peace and quiet. The assurance that you are with me. The joy of knowing you care for me and walk with me. How precious. Thank you, my Father. Oh, help my ears to listen and my heart to understand. Teach me your ways and lead me on in these years ahead. I do believe you have your plans for me, and I will meet with you each day to listen to your instruction as we plan the day ahead together.

GOD'S BLESSINGS FOR ME

"He who loves me will be loved by my Father,
and I too will love him and show myself to him."
JOHN 14:21B

FOR TODAY: Look for blessings and make blessings.

QUESTION TO CONSIDER: What blessings are ahead for me?

Father, I know you promised me blessings in my life. Now I am asking you to help me see them. I need someone right now that I can talk with about my dear husband. Someone I can weep with and laugh with and share my grief. I pray you will bring that person to me and we can be blessed by remembering so many things about him.

Whom can I find that I can weep with and laugh with now? Whom can I talk with about blessings in my life? What specifically do I want to talk about with that person?

_____

_____

_____

_____

_____

_____

_____

_____

_____

_____

_____

_____

_____

_____

_____

_____

_____

_____

_____

_____

_____

_____

_____

_____

_____

_____

_____

_____

_____

_____

"The Lord your God is with you, he is mighty to save. He will take great delight in you, he will quiet you with his love, he will rejoice over you with singing." Zephaniah 3:17

I think it is time I did something significant for a remembrance of him. Let me think of some options. I could plant a tree, a kind he liked. I could write a poem or even a story about him. I could put together a photo album just of his life. I could even buy myself a unique present, feeling in my soul that he would have done that as a gift to me.

Ah, one thing of importance I will do is have a memorial for him. A monument or a plaque with a message on it worthy of him. Yes, this is the time. I will make a choice so that his life will be remembered.

What are my options of things I could do as a special remembrance of my husband?

_____

_____

_____

_____

_____

_____

_____

_____

_____

_____

_____

_____

_____

_____

_____
_____
_____
_____
_____
_____
_____
_____
_____
_____
_____
_____
_____
_____
_____
_____
_____
_____
_____
_____
_____
_____
_____

"Precious in the sight of the Lord is the death of his saints."
Psalm 116:15

_____
date

That song of walking with the Lord in the garden is precious to me. What a comfort it is to simply close my eyes and walk with him in that garden. There is another old song that speaks to my heart and soul. It is called "Count Your Blessings." I must do this too.

> When upon life's billows you are tempest-tossed,
> When you are discouraged, thinking all is lost,
> Count your many blessings, name them one by one.
> And it will surprise you what the Lord hath done.
> Count your blessings, name them one by one;
> Count your many blessings, see what God hath done.

(Count Your Blessings, Johnson Oatman, Jr. pub. 1897)

I will write my blessings and name them one by one. Yes, here they are.

_____

_____

_____

_____

_____

_____

_____

_____

_____

_____

_____

_____

_____
_____
_____
_____
_____
_____
_____
_____
_____
_____
_____
_____
_____
_____
_____
_____
_____
_____
_____
_____

"Better is one day in your courts than a thousand elsewhere." Psalm 84:10
"O Lord Almighty, blessed is the man who trusts in you." Psalm 84:12

Yes, Father, help me find the way, the many ways, to count the blessings of having my husband in my life. And also your wonderful blessings and being with me through all of this grief and all the time. I want to count the blessings of today as well as yesterday. These all are gifts from you. Oh, how I thank you. You are with me all the time. Yes, you truly walk with me and you talk with me, and I am so blessed to be in your tender care.

There are so many blessings also from my family and my friends. They are the ones I can lean on, the ones I can weep with, the ones that pray for me and encourage me, the ones that have supplied all kinds of things for me during these difficult days. The ones I can talk with and share my feelings. The ones I can laugh with. The ones that are still my friends even though I am not a couple now but only a "one."

Here are some specific blessings from my family and friends.

_____

_____

_____

_____

_____

_____

_____

_____

_____

_____

_____

_____

_____

_____
_____
_____
_____
_____
_____
_____
_____
_____
_____
_____
_____
_____
_____
_____
_____
_____
_____
_____
_____
_____

Father, I thank you for the blessing you have given me, the care you have provided for me, the support that has come to me. What a mighty God you are to love me, care for me, and now walk with me through each of these days. I thank you and I honor you, my Lord and my God.

MY GRIEVING BODY

❦

"He gives strength to the weary and increases
the power of the weak … but those who hope
in the Lord will renew their strength. They will
soar on wings like eagles; they will run and not
grow weary, they will walk and not be faint."
ISAIAH 40:29,31

FOR TODAY: Healing my grieving body

QUESTIONS TO CONSIDER: Why does grief consume me physically, emotionally, cognitively, socially, and spiritually? What can I do about it?

Widows mourn their loss from the inside out. Everything, including my sleep patterns, is upset, out of control. I choose to stay on my side of the bed, where I have always slept. I choose to try to sleep as usual, but it doesn't always work. Going to sleep isn't easy anymore, and waking up is earlier even though these days my body needs more rest than usual. I find myself getting tired more quickly. I have lost the understanding of what each day holds and how it fits into my life. For sure, my body is having its own reaction to my grief.

My spirit needs you, Father, and my body certainly needs you too. Here is how my body is grieving.

_____

_____

_____

_____

_____

_____

_____

_____

_____

_____

_____

_____

_____

_____

_____

_____

_____

_____

_____

_____

_____

_____

_____

_____

_____

_____

_____

_____

_____

_____

"Even in laughter the heart may ache, and joy may end in grief."
Proverbs 14:13

Am I still important? Do I still count? Does my life matter? Thank you, Father, for helping me say "yes!" Yes, now is the time to take care of myself. Do I know what the future holds? No, but I must be prepared and take care of my physical body and look forward to what I can do and who I can be in due time. I don't need to know my future and I can't anyway, but I do need to keep this body in good shape so I can handle whatever comes my way. Yes, I will. This is my choice.

What plans can I make right now for how to care for this body of mine so I can make a difference and be prepared for the future?

_____

_____

_____

_____

_____

_____

_____

_____

_____

_____

_____

_____

_____

_____

_____

_____

_____

_____

_____

_____

_____

_____

_____

_____

_____

_____

_____

_____

_____

_____

_____

_____

_____

_____

_____

_____

_____

"The Sovereign Lord is my strength; he makes my feet like the feet of a deer, he enables me to go on the heights." Habakkuk 3:19

_____

Why do people tell me to be strong and keep busy? I am too tired and consumed to do that. Words like "just get busy" or "just put the past in the past" hurt and are discouraging. Actually this mourning process requires me to pay attention to my body, myself, to honor my body and take care of it so there will be a future for me. I am still alive, aren't I? I need a fresh spark to give my life meaning and purpose now. This is my problem, my challenge, and I must realize that I am the only one that can fix it.

So where do I find that spark? And what can I commit to do today and also in the weeks to come to help my body heal from grieving?

_____

_____

_____

_____

_____

_____

_____

_____

_____

_____

_____

_____

_____

_____

_____

_____

_____

_____

_____

_____

_____

_____

_____

_____

_____

_____

_____

_____

_____

_____

_____

_____

_____

_____

"So do not fear, for I am with you; do not be dismayed, for I am your God. I will strengthen you and help you; I will uphold you with my righteous right hand." Isaiah 41:10

_____

date

Checking with my doctor is essential. I need his council, his advice. It isn't only medical problems. I need him to tell me how best to stay strong mentally, physically, and emotionally. Or he can advise me as to who can help me. My pastor or church counselor would be a big help too. It is time for me to think about my future and my productivity for myself and others.

Here is my list of people to go to and talk with. And here is my list of some of the challenges I already know I need to work on.

_____

_____

_____

_____

_____

_____

_____

_____

_____

_____

_____

_____

_____

_____

_____

_____

_____

_____

_____

_____

_____

_____

_____

_____

_____

_____

_____

_____

_____

_____

_____

_____

_____

_____

_____

Here I am, Father. I submit my body to you. Lead me in these ideas you've given me so I can better serve you and have an even closer walk with you. Strengthen me so I can make a difference in other people's life. I am yours and you are mine.
Speak to me, Father. I am listening.

COMFORT WITH OTHERS

"Let us not love with words or tongue but with actions and in truth." 1 JOHN 3:18

FOR TODAY: Comfort for me, comfort for others

QUESTIONS TO CONSIDER: Are there others going through grief like I am? Where are they, and how can I meet them?

I would like to talk with others who are grieving. Other widows. See how they are handling their grief. Am I the only one who feels this way? My grief is so overwhelming. Is this normal, or am I going crazy? I need to find a support group and listen to others. I'll check with the church and see if there is a group. Maybe the hospital has one, and I am sure Hospice would have a support group. Yes, I can find others who are grieving. I can make a list of questions to ask others who have walked this path.

Why do I want a support group? How do I think a group will help me?

_____

_____

_____

_____

_____

_____

_____

_____

_____

_____

_____

_____

_____

_____

_____

_____

_____

_____

_____

_____

_____

_____

_____

_____

_____

_____

_____

_____

_____

_____

"The memory of the righteous will be a blessing." Proverbs 10:7

There are so many widows. I hear there are 11,000,000 in the U.S. alone. I am sure just talking with some will help me understand what I am going through better. It's time to make my list of questions to ask. One thing I want to know is how they feel each morning as they get out of bed. And another is how they handle phone calls for their husband. And just how do they process their grief?

Yes, how can I handle phone calls when the caller asks for my husband? If I'm not careful, I can be unkind with my reply. What is the best way to tell the caller that he has died? On the other hand, I don't want people, especially ones I don't have a close relationship with, to know that I am now living alone. It could make me vulnerable. I must write out a response so I am ready.

Here is my response so with the next call I will be ready with my answer.

_____

_____

_____

_____

_____

_____

_____

_____

_____

_____

_____

_____

_____

_____

_____

_____

_____

_____

_____

_____

_____

_____

_____

_____

_____

_____

_____

_____

_____

_____

_____

_____

_____

"The prayer of a righteous man is powerful and effective." James 5:16

—————
date

People say misery loves company. I'll see if it is true. I'll join a group and try it for two or three sessions and see if it works for me. It would be neat to have new friends that are in the middle of grief too. We could have so much to talk about, so much in common. They could be a comfort for me and I to them—and much better than doctors or lawyers or even clergy. On the other hand ....

What would I want to accomplish with a group? How could it help me?

_____

_____

_____

_____

_____

_____

_____

_____

_____

_____

_____

_____

_____

_____

_____

_____

_____

_____

_____

_____

_____

_____

_____

_____

_____

_____

_____

_____

_____

_____

_____

_____

_____

"Two are better than one, because they have a good return for their work: If one falls down, his friend can help him up. But pity the man who falls and has no one to help him up!" Ecclesiastes 4:9,10

I need to check with my church about a support group or check with another church. I have heard there are widow support groups, and I need one now. It could be a comfort to me, as we would understand our feelings. We could cry together and pray together. We could share some of our sorrows and learn how others are handling them. I need others, and a group too.

Where can I find a group like this to help me move forward and also understand my pain and loss?

_____

_____

_____

_____

_____

_____

_____

_____

_____

_____

_____

_____

_____

_____

_____

_____

_____

_____

_____

_____

_____

_____

_____

_____

_____

_____

_____

_____

_____

_____

_____

_____

_____

_____

_____

_____

_____

_____

Oh Father, how I thank you for giving me these thoughts. When I follow your direction, I not only help myself, but I can help others. I pray now that you will show me where to go and that I can even help other widows in this process.

YESTERDAY A WIFE, TODAY A MECHANIC

—— ✎ ——

"I can do everything through him who gives me strength." PHILIPPIANS 4:13

FOR TODAY: Becoming what I need to be

QUESTIONS TO CONSIDER: Just how do I repair that light fixture? And what do I do about that funny noise in the car?

I never had to replace a light fixture before, but now it is up to me. More problems keep coming. Now I realize how much I depended on my husband. Even those boxes in the trunk of the car seem too heavy for me. But it is either me who must deal with them or I must go find a friend that will help.

What are all those strange noises in the house? It seems the tick of the clock is different than I remember. Then there is that strange noise with the computer. And that new printer I just bought. Okay, how do I get it hooked up and working? Oh my, what do I do about these things I never expected to have to deal with?

Here is a list of those things I know will need attention sooner or later.

_____

_____

_____

_____

_____

_____

_____

_____

_____
_____
_____
_____
_____
_____
_____
_____
_____
_____
_____
_____
_____
_____
_____
_____
_____
_____

"Do not be anxious about anything, but in everything, by prayer and petition, with thanksgiving, present your requests to God."
Philippians 4:6

_____

date

Why is it so terribly difficult for me to open a jar, a can, a package, or even shrink-wrap? How in the world can I get that jar of pickles open? I used to just take it to my husband, but now that answer is gone. I've tried running hot water over the jar, using a gadget that is guaranteed to open anything but doesn't, and just deciding I didn't really want those pickles today anyway.

What about those "tamper-proof" pill bottles? They are made to protect children, but the manufacturers don't seem to realize I don't need that protection and I do need to get some of those pills out.

What are options that are realistic for dealing with these everyday activities?

_____

_____

_____

_____

_____

_____

_____

_____

_____

_____

_____

_____

_____

_____

_____

_____

_____

_____

_____

_____

_____

_____

_____

_____

_____

_____

_____

_____

_____

_____

_____

_____

_____

_____

"See, I am doing a new thing!" Isaiah 43:19

date

Where is my husband's toolbox? I will need some of his tools from time to time but not all of them. If he is like all other husbands I've heard of, he has about three of the same tool. I will lay them out and decide which ones would work best for me. Then I must find a special place for them so I will know where they are when I need them. I'll just give the rest of his tools to my kids, friends, or Goodwill. If they want them, I am a winner.

Here is my list of people to whom I can give tools. They were precious to him, so I do want to find a home for them.

_____

_____

_____

_____

_____

_____

_____

_____

_____

_____

_____

_____

_____

_____

_____

_____

_____

_____

_____

_____

_____

"Commit to the Lord whatever you do, and your plans will succeed."
Proverbs 16:3

How should I prepare for a storm or hurricane? I need to find out what radio station to listen to and become educated on how to be prepared if it is really going to be intense and a possible disaster. What in the house is essential to protect and keep? And how can I plan now to take care of these things? How do I protect the things I have outside? And do I have to do anything with my windows?

What do I do when a storm is actually coming? When storm warnings are on the TV, where do I go? And after the storm, I will have the "joy and privilege" of restoring everything. This will certainly be another challenge. Another time I will really need my husband and will miss him so very much. Time to get myself prepared now. "A prudent man sees danger and takes refuge" (Proverbs 22:3).

What do I need to do to prepare for a storm?

_____

_____

_____

_____

_____

_____

_____

_____

_____

_____

_____

_____

_____

Father, this is interesting. I never dreamed of these challenges and these decisions. How wonderful that you are always with me and can help me with all of them as well. Oh, what a blessing you are to me again and again and again.

THOSE HOLIDAYS

&ℒ

"I have learned to be content whatever the circumstances." PHILIPPIANS 4:11B

FOR TODAY: My plans for celebration times

QUESTION TO CONSIDER: What can I do to celebrate Thanksgiving, Christmas, Valentine's Day, Easter, and other special days?

Holidays will never be the same. How could they be without my husband, my children's dad? One thing is for sure, things change. Yes, they change all the time, and I just never expected all these changes.

So what do I do about Thanksgiving and Christmas? For sure I want to spend them with my family. How do I do that? I must plan ahead. I won't wait for something to happen. I'll make it happen. I'll ask what family members want to do this year and ask to be included. No, it won't be the same, but I'll start making new memories.

What are some options for Thanksgiving and Christmas this year? Let me make a list what I could do.

_____

_____

_____

_____

_____

_____

_____

_____

_____

_____

_____

_____

_____

_____

_____

_____

_____

_____

_____

_____

_____

_____

_____

_____

_____

_____

_____

_____

_____

_____

_____

_____

_____

_____

_____

"Forget the former things; do not dwell on the past." Isaiah 43:18

―――――――――
date

I've already decided what to do on my birthday this year. Of course, if one of my family members decides to help me celebrate, that is even better. More importantly, I need to offer to help all my family members with their birthday celebrations. I can do that. They are important to me, and here is my chance to serve, to bless, and to make their days a rich celebration. Why not?

Valentine's Day is a special day too, another one of the days I must work out now that I am alone. Maybe it would be more fun to send Valentines than to expect to receive them. Besides, if I send mine a bit early, maybe others will send me one too. At least I can buy a special one for me. One that I think my husband would pick out for me. And this may be the time to buy myself a few roses. Why not?

Let me make of list of all these holiday ideas and possibilities. I want to be the loving, caring woman that the Lord wants me to be.

―――――――――――――――――――――――――――――――

―――――――――――――――――――――――――――――――

―――――――――――――――――――――――――――――――

―――――――――――――――――――――――――――――――

―――――――――――――――――――――――――――――――

―――――――――――――――――――――――――――――――

―――――――――――――――――――――――――――――――

―――――――――――――――――――――――――――――――

―――――――――――――――――――――――――――――――

―――――――――――――――――――――――――――――――

―――――――――――――――――――――――――――――――

_____
_____
_____
_____
_____
_____
_____
_____
_____
_____
_____
_____
_____
_____
_____
_____
_____
_____
_____
_____
_____

"Give thanks in all circumstances, for this is God's will for you in Christ Jesus." 1 Thessalonians 5:18

Since I love to be with my family, maybe it is time for me to think of new ways of being together. I could plan a family reunion at a special place each year so we can all be together. A reunion would be a super time for us all to plan upcoming times together to remember certain years, Christmases, birthdays, special occasions, and even his funeral. A great time to bring out albums of old pictures. So many in my growing family haven't seen the old pictures, and they might even like to have copies.

Another great time would be for us all to go on a cruise together. There are Alaskan cruises, Caribbean cruises, and even longer ones around South America or in the Mediterranean. A week at a state park is a great idea too. Of course, these ideas will cost some dollars, but maybe we can all chip in somehow and make it happen.

Here is a list of ideas for times of celebration with my family that I think we can afford.

_____
_____
_____
_____
_____
_____
_____
_____
_____
_____
_____
_____
_____
_____
_____
_____
_____
_____
_____
_____

"Love the Lord, all his saints! The Lord preserves the faithful ... Be strong and take heart, all you who hope in the Lord."
Psalm 31:23,24

———————
date

Whenever a new baby joins our family, we could have a special welcoming party. Those grandchildren and great grandchildren are wonderful. Now I know why they are called great, since they are so special. What a neat time to take pictures too.

We could even make a special gathering to remember the day our loved one has his birthday in heaven. We could make it a joyful time, knowing he is having the ultimate rewards from this life. It would be a comfort for me to have family with me on that day.

Here is a list of things I can work on and plan for myself and for my family.

_____

_____

_____

_____

_____

_____

_____

_____

_____

_____

_____

_____

_____

_____

_____
_____
_____
_____
_____
_____
_____
_____
_____
_____
_____
_____
_____
_____
_____
_____
_____
_____
_____

Oh Father, what a blessing that you are always, yes always with me. You are eternal. You care of me. You have your plans for me. Here I am. Help me to listen to you and think your thoughts and plan what you have in mind. I am leaning on you, and I thank you for your love and special care for me.

FORWARD WITH CONFIDENCE

—————— ✿ ——————

"The Lord is my shepherd, I shall not be in want. He
makes me lie down in green pastures, he leads me
beside quiet waters, he restores my soul. He guides
me in paths of righteousness for his name's sake."

PSALM 23:1-3

FOR TODAY: A whole world of choices ahead for me

QUESTIONS TO CONSIDER: What do I do with all my time and the
many choices I have to use it wisely?

At this stage of my life, I can see many things I could do. Some of
my friends like to play bridge or euchre. Some others are into golf or
tennis. These are certainly some options.

My sister-in-law decided to go back to work rather than be home
alone. There are lots of work opportunities I could look into if work is
really what I want to do. I don't have to have an important job, just one
where I can work each day, help, and get a paycheck.

My neighbor volunteers at the hospital. I know the staff at the Shelter
for the Poor downtown always needs help. There are opportunities at
church too.

*Here is my list of some of my widow friends and what they are doing
with their time.*

_____

_____

_____

_____

_____

_____

221

_____

_____

_____

_____

_____

_____

_____

_____

_____

_____

_____

_____

_____

_____

_____

_____

_____

_____

_____

_____

_____

"But seek first his kingdom and his righteousness, and all these things will be given to you as well. Therefore do not worry about tomorrow, for tomorrow will worry about itself." Matthew 6:33,34

My husband and I used to enjoy making long-range plans. We were always thinking of what we wanted to do in the next five years or ten years. Some of those plans we were able to do. Some just never happened. Things changed.

Change comes ever faster now. There is so much change I really can't count on what the world will be like in ten years. And certainly this singleness that I am experiencing is a change I didn't anticipate.

Now I am to think about my plans. I am to plan for the future but not at the expense of the present. Every new day presents new surprises. Proverbs 27:1 tells me, "Do not boast about tomorrow, for you do not know what a day may bring forth." This advice certainly is true with the stock market, with our economy, with our country's international relations—even with all the internationals that now live in our area. Always change and more change.

What are some of the significant changes I have seen in these last years that already affect or may soon affect the way I do things as a widow?

_____

_____

_____

_____

_____

_____

_____

_____

_____

_____

_____
_____
_____
_____
_____
_____
_____
_____
_____
_____
_____
_____
_____
_____
_____
_____
_____
_____
_____
_____
_____
_____

*"I will sing of the Lord's great love forever; with my mouth I will make
your faithfulness known through all generations."
Psalm 89:1*

I must remember the Lord does have his plans for me. He does want me to be useful to him. In Mark 1:17 Jesus saw Andrew and told him to come follow him and he would make him a disciple. That call was certainly all new to Andrew, who was a fisherman, but Andrew chose to follow Jesus anyway. Okay, Father, what do you want me to do?

I heard of a widow who is now speaking in churches and teaching children and adults. There is another, with her skills on the piano, who is a volunteer for a church. Then one widow who had never written a book before is now writing her fourth book. Interesting.

Some are major caregivers for their grandchildren. That would be an enjoyable time, but it might also be too controlling of one's time. Another widow is now hiring her services in caring for an invalid by working with a service company. That, too, would take a huge time commitment.

Let me make my list of all the possibilities I could choose, whether they are the best or not. They are possibilities, opportunities.

_____

_____

_____

_____

_____

_____

_____

_____

_____

_____

_____

_____
_____
_____
_____
_____
_____
_____
_____
_____
_____
_____
_____
_____
_____
_____
_____
_____
_____
_____
_____
_____
_____

*"Being confident of this, that he who began a good work within
you will carry it on to completion until the day of Christ Jesus."
Philippians 1:6*

I have heard the expression "think outside the box." Looks like this is one of the things I should do now. Here I am with skills and time, and I certainly can be useful in some way. Actually I could look at this time in my life like teenagers do, trying to decide what they want to do when they grow up. My advantage over teenagers is that I have more experience and understanding just because I have all those years behind me, years with hard earned knowledge.

To help me "think outside the box" for my life, I'll ask these chosen friends what possibilities they see for me.

_____

_____

_____

_____

_____

_____

_____

_____

_____

_____

_____

_____

_____

_____

_____

_____

_____

_____

_____

_____

_____

_____

_____

_____

_____

_____

_____

_____

_____

_____

_____

_____

_____

_____

_____

_____

_____

_____

Here I am, Father, needing you guidance and direction. I want to use my days as you want me to. I want to be useful to you. It will certainly be a joy to be able to help other people in whatever way you prepare for me. Here I am, Father. Show me your plan and your direction for my life today and my future.

BUILDING A LEGACY

"Give thanks in all circumstances, for this is God's will for you in Christ Jesus."
1 THESSALONIANS 5:18

FOR TODAY: Making a legacy of all those past "circumstances"

QUESTION TO CONSIDER: How do I help my children, my grandchildren, and even my great grandchildren understand and value the heritage they have received from their ancestors?

Many chapters in the Old Testament speak of the legacy the children of Abraham, Isaiah, and Jacob received. Likewise, the Old Testament tells of the blessings of King David's life and how his offspring were chosen to bless the world with the birth of Jesus. The New Testament tells how the ministries of the apostles affected their world, and their stories still challenge each of us to follow their instructions and guidance.

Looks like it is time to see about the legacy that I am going to pass on to my family. We know about these blessings in the Bible because they were written and preserved for us. Maybe it is time to write my stories too so that they can be read and remembered.

What stories would I like to write about my husband?

_____

_____

_____

_____

_____

_____

_____

_____

_____

_____

_____

_____

_____

_____

_____

_____

_____

_____

_____

_____

_____

_____

_____

_____

_____

_____

_____

"Posterity will serve him; future generations will be told about the Lord. They will proclaim his righteousness to a people yet unborn—for he has done it." Psalm 22: 30,31

It will be important for my children to know about their dad's parents and grandparents too, and what it was like growing up in those days. Their great grandparents also have history that can be recorded. It would be good for my children to know how much education their ancestors had, what kind of work they did, and what countries they were from originally. And what are the blessings of my husband's family that have been passed down to today?

I have stories about my life too and of my ancestors. I need to write them as well. There are stories of my grandparents and great grandparents. They certainly lived in a different world. There are their stories about WW II, the Korean War, the war in Vietnam. Each of these wars had different effects on the country and my ancestors.

I can write all of these stories and make a small book with them. I can find a shop to help me put all these stories together.

What resources do I need in order to do this project?

_____

_____

_____

_____

_____

_____

_____

_____

_____

_____

_____

_____

_____

_____

_____

_____

_____

_____

_____

_____

_____

_____

_____

_____

_____

_____

_____

_____

_____

_____

_____

_____

_____

"Even when I am old and gray, do not forsake me, O God, till I declare your power to the next generation, your might to all who are to come."
Psalm 71:18

My photos are so special and significant too. Each one means so very much. They need to be placed in special albums with explanations for each one. Yes, the names, place, occasion, and year for each one. Those albums could be a big help for the family in understanding some of the important events and gatherings of the past and what they meant to my husband and me.

The pictures of our childhood look so ancient now. And they really are. The clothes are different, the adults look so strange, and the location in most of them is unknown. And look at my wedding pictures. Weddings today don't look the same, but mine shows the special ways we did things then.

I have pictures of the different stages of my life and his life. It will be a joy and pleasure to prepare them in albums too so they will be a lasting heritage for this wonderful family of mine. How special to me. And how special it will be for them. I need to write the date on these pictures and lay them out according in order.

What can I do to make my family value these pictures and enjoy them?

_____

_____

_____

_____

_____

_____

_____

_____

_____

_____

_____
_____
_____
_____
_____
_____
_____
_____
_____
_____
_____
_____
_____
_____
_____
_____
_____
_____
_____

"Know therefore that the Lord you God is God; he is the faithful God, keeping his covenant of love to a thousand generations of those who love him and keep his commands." Deuteronomy 7:9

Of course there were special times and events too. Maybe I could make a list of the key points in our life. Times of great significance. I certainly remember the times when we bought a new car or a new house. And our family vacation times. And those special days when the children were sent off to college.

Maybe I could plan a Heritage Celebration. That could turn into a great occasion. Memory time for everyone. Maybe I could even write up a quiz game using many of the past blessings and see who can remember the most. It could be a wonderful time of remembering the blessings of our heritage. It could also help everyone understand the blessings our family has been given over the years.

Here is my list of the many things I might do to help my family know and remember the blessings of all those who were before them.

———————————————————————————

———————————————————————————

———————————————————————————

———————————————————————————

———————————————————————————

———————————————————————————

———————————————————————————

———————————————————————————

———————————————————————————

———————————————————————————

———————————————————————————

———————————————————————————

_____

_____

_____

_____

_____

_____

_____

_____

_____

_____

_____

_____

_____

_____

_____

_____

_____

_____

_____

Oh Father, how I thank you, how I praise you for your love and care for me over the years. I have been blessed by my heritage. Yes, there have been some bad times, but you have always been there for all of us. Now I praise you and thank you for being my Heavenly Father and for the precious heritage you have for all of us as we accept you to be our Father. I want to always praise you and thank you for your blessings.

LIVING IN THE NOW, TODAY

"This is the day the Lord has made so I will rejoice and be glad in it." PSALM 118:24

FOR TODAY: Living in the world of today

QUESTIONS TO CONSIDER: What do I do in the "now"? Where should I focus my life, my time, my service?

Answering these questions is significant. Let's see. Looking at my age and guessing as to how many years I have ahead, I have some significant choices to make.

Yes, the past is important, but this is the time to look at the present. What does today hold? I must learn how I can enjoy today. Yes today. Jude 20,21 says, "Build yourselves up in your most holy faith ... Keep yourselves in God's love as you wait for the mercy of our Lord Jesus Christ to bring you to eternal life." How wonderful to claim this verse for today.

What a joy to be available to the Lord for service. First let me list the ways I have served him in the past.

_____

_____

_____

_____

_____

_____

_____

_____

_____

_____

_____

_____

_____

_____

_____

_____

_____

_____

_____

_____

_____

_____

_____

_____

_____

_____

_____

_____

"Teach me your way, O Lord; lead me in a straight path."
Psalm 27:11

Now is the time to enjoy each morning. The sunshine and the rain. The many and varied gifts from God to this world. The seasons speak of his beauty. The variety of trees, flowers, plants, animals, and all speak of his majesty. All through the Bible he is telling of his love and his desire to lead me through each day.

Now is the time to appreciate and love my family and my heritage. They have helped make me who I am today. Now is also the time to appreciate and love my friends. Those close ones who have stood with me through my trauma and my sorrow.

Now is the time to appreciate my possessions, the roof over my head and the food on my table plus all those special things I have collected across the years that are still meaningful to me.

Here are some things that make today special and that I enjoy today, yes, now.

_____

_____

_____

_____

_____

_____

_____

_____

_____

_____

_____

_____

_____

_____
_____
_____
_____
_____
_____
_____
_____
_____
_____
_____
_____
_____
_____
_____
_____
_____
_____
_____
_____

"When you have eaten and are satisfied, praise the Lord you God."
Deuteronomy 8:10

---
date

NOW is important. TODAY is where I am. I have all the choices of being happy, sad, content, pleased, angry, disturbed, frustrated, and joyful. They are mine to choose. And the Lord has told me how to live each day. He orders my steps, and I can choose the joy of following him. He gives me the Holy Spirit so I can produce his fruit

> of *love*, a gift
> of *joy*, which I must search for
> of *peace,* and how comforting it is
> of *patience,* and I do need it
> of *kindness*, and the privilege of being kind
> of *goodness,* which is what I have been taught
> of *faithfulness,* that I learn from his Word
> of *gentleness,* with his caring spirit

I must remember the fruits of the spirit today and enjoy having them and sharing them with others. It will be a special joy this evening when I bow before the Lord and thank him for enjoying the NOW of today.

Here are my thoughts on the NOW of today.

_____

_____

_____

_____

_____

_____

_____

_____

_____

_____

_____

_____

_____

_____

_____

_____

_____

_____

_____

_____

_____

_____

_____

_____

_____

_____

_____

_____

_____

_____

_____

_____

_____

_____

"Praise be to the Lord, for he showed his wonderful love to me."
Psalm 31:21

_____
date

NOW I can choose to praise you, Lord, and thank you for your blessings.
NOW I can sing a new song to you.
NOW I can ask for your guidance and blessings for this day.
NOW I can thank you and worship you.
NOW I can go forth with joy.
NOW I know that I am your child and you are my Heavenly Father.

*"Praise the Lord, O my soul; all my inmost being, praise his holy name.
Praise the Lord, O my soul, and forget not all his benefits." Psalm 103:1,2*

Oh Father, what am I to do to be living in your joy today, now?

_____

_____

_____

_____

_____

_____

_____

_____

_____

_____

_____

_____

_____

_____

_____

_____
_____
_____
_____
_____
_____
_____
_____
_____
_____
_____
_____
_____
_____
_____
_____
_____
_____
_____
_____

My Heavenly Father, thank you for enabling me to enjoy today, to listen to you today, to know that you are with me today. Thank you that I can move from the past to the NOW and all that you have for me.

LIVING FOR THE FUTURE

"God has given us eternal life, and this life is in his Son. He who has the Son has life; he who does not have the Son of God does not have life."

1 JOHN 5:11,12

FOR TODAY: Heaven and eternity

QUESTIONS TO CONSIDER: What does the ultimate future look like? What can I expect?

What a joy, what a comfort to know we will be in heaven when we die. Jesus, you told us in John 14:6, "I am the way and the truth and the life. No one comes to the Father except through me." And since I have followed your instruction, I have that assurance.

What a relief and blessing it is to know you, Heavenly Father, are in charge of this world. You are the one who made heaven and earth. You are the one who told us how to live so we could be with you through all eternity. It is all written down for us in your Word, and when we become your children, we can claim our eternal future with you.

What would I like heaven to be like?

_____

_____

_____

_____

_____

_____

_____

_____

_____
_____
_____
_____
_____
_____
_____
_____
_____
_____
_____
_____
_____
_____
_____
_____
_____
_____
_____
_____
_____
_____

*"Blessed are those who wash their robes, that they may have the
right to the tree of life and may go through the gates into the city."*
Revelation 22:14

————————
date

I hear that the streets of heaven are pure gold and that you, Father, have prepared a mansion for me. It must be difficult for you to have to use words we know in order to explain things in heaven to us. But the words you use such as *gold* and *mansion* are surely not the same things in heaven.

The more I read the book of John, the more I realize God has his plans for me to join him in heaven. All I have to do is to just follow Jesus and I will get there.

I don't know who will meet me at the Pearly Gate, but I will certainly be looking for my dear husband. I like to imagine that he'll meet me with a kiss and a hug.

Here is what I want to see when I enter heaven. Here is what I want to do.

_____

_____

_____

_____

_____

_____

_____

_____

_____

_____

_____

_____

_____

_____
_____
_____
_____
_____
_____
_____
_____
_____
_____
_____
_____
_____
_____
_____
_____
_____
_____
_____
_____
_____
_____

"For you granted him (Jesus) authority over all people that he might give eternal life to all those you have given him." John 17:2

—————
date

Yes, I have mourned the death of my dear husband. I miss him so, and I know I always will. And I know my family will mourn my death too. Part of this mourning is because we only see life here on earth and can't envision heaven and all the joy and pleasure it will be to be there with our Heavenly Father and our Christian family.

I want to do all I can to prepare for my final journey, my passage to heaven. And I want to make my passing from this life to the next as easy as possible on my family. Now is the time to lay out plans my family can follow when I am gone from them like my husband is gone from me.

Here is information they will need and where it is located. My will, my bank, credit cards, life insurance, real estate holdings, financial assets, social security information, power of attorney, and bequests. I'll write it all here, and then I will make a copy and file it so they can find it easily when I am gone.

_____

_____

_____

_____

_____

_____

_____

_____

_____

_____

_____

_____

_____
_____
_____
_____
_____
_____
_____
_____
_____
_____
_____
_____
_____
_____
_____
_____
_____
_____
_____
_____
_____
_____

*"Well done, good and faithful servant! You have been faithful with a
few things ... Come and share your master's happiness!"*
Matthew 25:21

_____
date

I can write my ideas for my funeral too. No, not a funeral. It is to be a CELEBRATION. I can certainly write out my words for them to hear. Words that tell them the Lord is my Savior and he is the one who will open heaven's door for me. I want to write words that will be a blessing to them. I can share with them my feelings, my assurance, and my expectations for my eternal home in heaven. Yes, yes, yes. Yes, I can do this.

Here are the things I want to do to make the celebration of my journey to heaven a blessing to my family and friends. And here is my testimony of the presence of the Lord God Almighty in my life.

_____

_____

_____

_____

_____

_____

_____

_____

_____

_____

_____

_____

_____

_____

_____

_____

_____

_____

_____

_____

_____

_____

_____

_____

_____

_____

_____

_____

_____

_____

_____

_____

_____

Oh Father, when I think of the future, when I think of the blessing of eternal life with you, it is all beyond my comprehension. I know you do care for me every day. You do forgive my sins and make me your blessed child. How precious this is. My trust is in you, Jesus, because you told me to not let my heart be troubled and to trust you. You said you are preparing a place for me. You give me strength and assurance, and I know you will be with me today, tomorrow, and all the days of my life. What blessed assurance! How I praise you! How I thank you! Oh, I worship you, my Lord and my God. Help me live this day and every day of my life in service to you. Amen.

Title: _____

date _____

This is not the time to quit. Carry on and write your own chapters, your continuing letters to your Heavenly Father, on the pages that follow. He has so very much ahead for you, and he wants to hear from you with your prayers and your letters. May God bless you each and every day.

_____

_____

_____

_____

_____

_____

_____

_____

_____

_____

_____

_____

_____

_____

_____

_____

_____

_____

Title: _____

date _____

_____

_____

_____

_____

_____

_____

_____

_____

_____

_____

_____

_____

_____

_____

_____

_____

_____

_____

_____

Title: _____
date _____

_____

_____

_____

_____

_____

_____

_____

_____

_____

_____

_____

_____

_____

_____

_____

_____

_____

_____

Title: _____
date _____

_____
_____
_____
_____
_____
_____
_____
_____
_____
_____
_____
_____
_____
_____
_____
_____
_____
_____
_____
_____
_____

Title: _____
date _____

_____

_____

_____

_____

_____

_____

_____

_____

_____

_____

_____

_____

_____

_____

_____

_____

_____

_____

Title: _____
date _____

_____

_____

_____

_____

_____

_____

_____

_____

_____

_____

_____

_____

_____

_____

_____

_____

_____

_____

_____

Title: _____
date _____

_____

_____

_____

_____

_____

_____

_____

_____

_____

_____

_____

_____

_____

_____

_____

_____

_____

_____

Title: _____

date _____

_____

_____

_____

_____

_____

_____

_____

_____

_____

_____

_____

_____

_____

_____

_____

_____

_____

_____

_____

Title: _____
date _____

_____

_____

_____

_____

_____

_____

_____

_____

_____

_____

_____

_____

_____

_____

_____

_____

_____

Title: _____
date _____

_____

_____

_____

_____

_____

_____

_____

_____

_____

_____

_____

_____

_____

_____

_____

_____

_____

_____

_____

LIVING FOR THE FUTURE

Title: _____
date _____

_____
_____
_____
_____
_____
_____
_____
_____
_____
_____
_____
_____
_____
_____
_____
_____
_____
_____

Title: _____

date _____

_____

_____

_____

_____

_____

_____

_____

_____

_____

_____

_____

_____

_____

_____

_____

_____

_____

_____

_____

Title: _____
date _____

_____

_____

_____

_____

_____

_____

_____

_____

_____

_____

_____

_____

_____

_____

_____

_____

_____

_____

Title: _____

date _____

Title: _____
date _____

_____
_____
_____
_____
_____
_____
_____
_____
_____
_____
_____
_____
_____
_____
_____
_____
_____
_____
_____

Title: _____
date _____

Title: _____

date _____

_____

_____

_____

_____

_____

_____

_____

_____

_____

_____

_____

_____

_____

_____

_____

_____

_____

Title: _____
date _____

_____

_____

_____

_____

_____

_____

_____

_____

_____

_____

_____

_____

_____

_____

_____

_____

_____

_____

_____

_____

Title: _____

date _____

_____

_____

_____

_____

_____

_____

_____

_____

_____

_____

_____

_____

_____

_____

_____

_____

_____

Title: _____
date _____

_____

_____

_____

_____

_____

_____

_____

_____

_____

_____

_____

_____

_____

_____

_____

_____

_____

_____

_____

_____

26134476R00176

Made in the USA
Charleston, SC
25 January 2014